EYEWITNESS
SHAKESPEARE

Quill pens

Hornbook

Horn inkwells

Nine men's morris game

Boy player

Hautboy, or shawm

Model of the Globe Theatre

Hare

Schoolboy

Spanish galleon

Skull used as a prop

EYEWITNESS
SHAKESPEARE

Written by
PETER CHRISP

Photographed by
STEVE TEAGUE

**Swordfighting
in *Hamlet***

Black rat

Crown used
as a prop

Rooster
used in
cockfights

Traveling
library

Sword and
dagger

Bunch of
garden
herbs

Bottom from
*A Midsummer
Night's Dream*

Elizabethan
noblewoman

DK | Penguin
Random
House

Project editor Louise Pritchard
Art editor Jill Plank
Editor Annabel Blackledge
Assistant art editors Kate Adams, Yolanda Carter
Senior editor Monica Byles
Senior art editors Jane Tetzlaff, Clare Shedden
Category publisher Jayne Parsons
Senior managing art editor Jacquie Gulliver
Senior production controller Kate Oliver
Picture researcher Franziska Marking
Picture librarians Sally Hamilton, Rachel Hilford
DTP designers Matthew Ibbotson, Justine Eaton
Jacket designer Dean Price

RELAUNCH EDITION (DK UK)
Editor Ashwin Khurana
US editor Margaret Parrish
Managing editor Gareth Jones
Managing art editor Philip Letsu
Publisher Andrew Macintyre
Producer, pre-production Adam Stoneham
Senior producer Janis Griffith
Jacket editor Maud Whatley
Jacket designer Laura Brim
Jacket design development manager Sophia MTT
Publishing director Jonathan Metcalf
Associate publishing director Liz Wheeler
Art director Phil Ormerod

RELAUNCH EDITION (DK INDIA)
Editor Ishani Nandi
Project art editor Deep Shikha Walia
Art editor Amit Varma
DTP designer Pawan Kumar
Senior DTP designer Harish Aggarwal
Managing editor Alka Thakur Hazarika
Managing art editor Romi Chakraborty
CTS manager Balwant Singh
Jacket designers Suhita Dharamjit, Sukriti Sobti
Managing jacket editor Saloni Singh

First American Edition, 2002
This American Edition, 2015
Published in the United States by DK Publishing
345 Hudson Street, New York, New York 10014

A catalog record for this book is
available from the Library of Congress.

ISBN 978-1-4654-3185-1 (PB)

ISBN 978-1-4654-3361-9 (ALB)

DK books are available at special discounts
when purchased in bulk for sales promotions,
premiums, fund-raising, or educational use.
For details, contact: DK Publishing Special
Markets, 345 Hudson Street, New York, New
York 10014 or SpecialSales@dk.com.

Color reproduction by
Alta Image Ltd, London, UK

Printed and bound by
South China Printing Co. Ltd., China

All images ©
Dorling Kindersley Limited

For further information see:
www.dkimages.com

A WORLD OF IDEAS:
SEE ALL THERE IS TO KNOW

Contents

Lute

The early years

William Shakespeare was born in 1564 in the market town of Stratford-upon-Avon, England. His exact birth date is unknown, but it would have been shortly before his christening on April 26. William was born into a wealthy middle-class family. His father, John, served on the town council and was one of Stratford's leading men. He worked as a glove-maker, and also dealt in wool and lumber.

Shakespeare's birthplace
William was born in this house in Henley Street, Stratford. The house is now the Birthplace Museum and is furnished as it would have been in Shakespeare's day.

16th-century civic maces

Position of authority
In 1568, John Shakespeare was high bailiff of Stratford, which was similar to being a mayor. His authority was symbolized by an ornamental staff called a mace.

Leftovers for sale
John Shakespeare bought sheepskins from the butchers to make his gloves. He cut away the sheep's wool, then sold it to Stratford's dyers and weavers. It was dyed using a variety of local plants and woven into cloth.

Maces were originally used as weapons

Blue dye came from the woad plant

Yellow dye came from the weld plant, or "dyer's broom"

Red dye came from madder roots

16th-century velvet and satin mittens embroidered with flowers

Glove story
In the 16th century, wealthy people wore beautifully embroidered gloves like these mittens. John would not have sewn them himself. Embroidery was done mainly in the home by women.

Henley Street
John Shakespeare's workshop was located in his house in Henley Street. Here, he cut and sewed the animal skins into gloves.

Walls were covered with decorative tapestries or cheaper painted cloth

Straw was used as a mattress

Crowded house
William probably shared a trundle bed like this with some of his brothers and sisters. During the day, the lower bed could be wheeled under the upper one.

Mother's room
This is thought to be the room where John's wife Mary gave birth to William and his seven brothers and sisters. A cradle stands by the bed, and the basket is full of linen strips used to wrap babies.

Knobs and grooves carved by hand

Built to impress
As a small child, William probably sat in an elaborately carved high chair just like this. Parents who could afford such a fancy high chair would be seen to have wealth and good taste.

Family misfortunes
For a time, John Shakespeare's businesses were very successful, and he could afford expensive tableware like these pewter dishes. However, in 1576, when William was 12 years old, John got into debt and lost his position of importance in the town.

Going to school

Birch twigs
Schoolmasters always carried a bundle of birch twigs. This was used to beat pupils when they misbehaved.

At about the age of four, William Shakespeare would have gone to a "petty school" to learn to read. This was a small private school for boys and girls. At six, the girls left school to be taught at home, while middle-class boys like William went on to the local grammar school to learn Latin. At the time, people needed to know Latin if they wanted to follow a career in law, medicine, teaching, or the Church.

Pater noster qui es in caelis ÷ Sanctificetur nomen tuum ÷ Adveniat regnum tuum ÷ Fiat voluntas tua sicut in caelo et in terra ÷ Panem nostrum quotidianum da nobis hodie ÷ Et dimitte nobis debita nostra sicut et nos dimittimus debitoribus nostris ÷ Et ne nos inducas in temptatione ÷ Sed libera nos a malo ÷ Amen ÷

Reading matters
Children learned to read using a "hornbook," a piece of wood covered with printed paper, protected by a sheet of transparent horn.

Hornbook containing the words from the Lord's Prayer in Latin

With his hornbook and satchel, the boy sets off to school

Reluctant pupils
Most boys hated going to school. The hours were long, the classes were dull, and their behavior was strictly controlled.

19th-century painting illustrating Jaques's speech about a whining schoolboy in *As You Like It*

Feathers tended to get in the way, but were sometimes left on for show

"And then the whining schoolboy, with his satchel, and shining morning face, creeping like a snail unwillingly to school."

WILLIAM SHAKESPEARE
JAQUES IN *AS YOU LIKE IT*

The pen had to be dipped into the ink at regular intervals

Pen and ink

Pupils had to make themselves a pen called a quill from a goose feather. They cut the tip of the feather at an angle to make a nib. Ink was kept in an inkwell made of horn, wood, pottery, or metal.

Horn inkwells

Balancing act

There were no desks, so pupils had to rest their work on their knees. This was no problem when they were reading from text books, but it must have been difficult when they had to practice their handwriting!

A selection of goose-feather quills

Tragic inspiration

At school, Shakespeare read the works of ancient Roman authors like Seneca, who wrote plays about suffering and death. One of Shakespeare's first plays was *Titus Andronicus*, a bloodthirsty tragedy inspired by Seneca.

Old favorite

One of Shakespeare's favorite writers was the poet Ovid (43 BCE–17 CE), whose poem *Metamorphoses* is a collection of stories drawn from ancient Greek and Roman myths.

As he reads, the schoolboy follows the words with his finger

Religious conflict

The 16th century was a time of bitter religious conflict. All English people were Christian, but there were two rival versions of the faith—Catholicism and Protestantism. In 1534, Henry VIII broke with the Pope and the Catholic Church. His son Edward VI and younger daughter Elizabeth I supported the Protestant faith, while his elder daughter Mary was a devout Catholic.

Mary, crowned Queen of Heaven, holds the baby Jesus

An English Bible
Catholics used a Latin Bible, but Protestants thought that the Bible should be translated. This English translation was written in Switzerland during Mary's reign.

Queen of Heaven
Catholics prayed in front of statues of saints, such as Mary the mother of Christ, whom they called the Queen of Heaven. Protestants claimed that religious statues were idols. Under the Protestant king, Edward VI, statues like this were smashed to pieces.

Counting prayers
Catholics used rosary beads to keep count of prayers. They believed that repeating certain Latin prayers would help them to get to heaven.

Carrying case made of leather

Chalice for giving wine at communion

Plate for communion wafers

Christ depicted on the cross

Communion
Catholics believed that priests could turn bread and wine into the body and blood of Christ. Priests carried communion sets like this to perform the ceremony for Catholics worshiping in secret.

Bottle for carrying wine

Bloody Mary

Queen Mary was nicknamed "Bloody Mary" because she had almost 290 Protestants burned at the stake. In turn, Elizabeth I had 193 Catholics executed because they were loyal to the Pope.

The lamb, a sacrificial animal, stands for Christ, whom Christians believe sacrificed himself to save humanity

Simple cross

Richly decorated Catholic cross

At the ends of the cross are portraits of Matthew, Mark, Luke, and John

A Puritan father gives his family religious instruction

Puritan beliefs

The Puritans were strict Protestants who believed that the break with the Catholic Church had not gone far enough. They wanted to get rid of bishops, church clothes, and all elaborate ceremonies.

Catholic plots

In 1587, Queen Elizabeth I had her cousin, Mary Queen of Scots, executed. Mary, a Catholic, was beheaded after a series of plots by English Catholics who planned to kill Elizabeth I and make Mary queen. Such plots were encouraged by the Pope, the head of the Catholic Church, who had declared in 1570 that Elizabeth I was no longer the rightful queen.

Mixed beliefs

Catholics and Protestants both used the cross as a symbol of their faith, though Catholic crosses were more ornate. It is hard to tell what Shakespeare believed. His plays do show certain Catholic features, such as characters that swear by saints. However, one play, *King John,* is strongly anti-Catholic. Perhaps, like many English people, he had a mixture of beliefs.

11

A country childhood

William Shakespeare grew up in the heart of the countryside. He knew the farmers' fields around Stratford, the meadows where wild flowers grew, and the Forest of Arden to the north. As an adult writing plays in London, Shakespeare drew on his memories of the countryside. His plays are full of accurate descriptions of birds, flowers, trees, wild animals, clouds, and the changing seasons.

Fields of France
As a boy, Shakespeare would often have seen oxen plowing the fields. In *Henry V*, he compares France to an unplowed field overgrown with weeds.

Longhorn

Little livestock
Farm animals were smaller in Shakespeare's time. Some of today's rare breeds, like the Bagot goat, give us an idea of what they looked like.

Livestock

In the 1500s, farm animals had many uses. Cattle were milked and used to pull plows. Goats and sheep provided wool, meat, milk, horn, and leather. In November, when stocks of animal feed were low, pigs were fed on acorns, to provide a source of fresh meat for winter.

"When icicles hang by the wall, And Dick the shepherd blows his nail, And Tom bears logs into the hall, And milk comes frozen home in pail..."

WILLIAM SHAKESPEARE
WINTER IN *LOVE'S LABOUR'S LOST*

Bagot goat

Pitchfork, for moving piles of hay, straw, and harvested cereal

Wheat

Daily bread
Cereals were grown to make bread. Expensive bread was made from wheat, while cheaper bread was made from barley and rye. If the crops failed, people ate bread made from oats.

Oats   Rye   Barley

Crops and flowers

Country life in Shakespeare's day was a never-ending cycle of plowing, sowing, and harvesting. Nothing was wasted—even wild flowers and plants were harvested for use in cooking, medicine, and the home. Shakespeare used images of crops, plants, and wild flowers to bring his writing to life.

Crook, to hold stalks together when harvesting

Harvesttime
Tools, such as crooks and sickles, were used to harvest crops. Cereals were loaded on to a wagon with a pitchfork, then taken away to be threshed, or beaten.

Sickle, used to cut crops

Peasant's cart

Cowslip

Nettle

Bristles cover the whole body

Pig

Posies and poisons
Shakespeare wrote about flowers in many of his plays. In *Hamlet*, Ophelia makes garlands of "crow flowers, nettles, daisies and long purples." The wicked queen in *Cymbeline* plots to make poison from primroses, violets, and cowslips.

Sweet violet

Primrose

Illustration of Ophelia by Walter Crane, 1906

Country fun

In the countryside around Stratford, people made their own entertainment. They kicked balls made from pigs' bladders, practiced archery, and played simple board games. The wild creatures in the fields and forests provided locals with sport, as well as meat. The poor hunted small birds and animals, while the wealthy chased larger prey, such as wild boar and deer.

Hunting wild boar was a dangerous sport

The hood stopped the bird from flying away

Gyrfalcon

Hunting

Hunting and falconry (hunting using birds of prey) were popular pastimes. Nobles kept peregrine falcons and gyrfalcons for catching pigeons, ducks, herons, and rooks. Poorer people kept goshawks, which were used to hunt hares, rabbits, and partridges.

Hare, hunted mainly for its meat

Dost thou love hawking?

A lord in *The Taming of the Shrew* asks "Dost thou love hawking?" Shakespeare certainly did and often mentions it in his plays. In *Romeo and Juliet,* the heroine cries to her departing lover, "O! for a falconer's voice, to lure this tassel-gentle back again." A tassel-gentle was a male peregrine falcon.

Mastiff dog, used to kill wild boar

The falconer gripped the jesses, or leather straps, attached to the bird's legs

Bloodhound, used to sniff out wild boar and deer

Swift greyhound, used for coursing (running after hares)

Hunting hounds

Various types of dog were bred for hunting. Greyhounds were bred for speed. In *Henry VI, Part Three,* Queen Margaret compares the enemies following her to two greyhounds chasing a hare.

Jingling bells allowed the falconer to find the bird when it went out of sight

A heavy glove protected the hand from the bird's sharp talons

Backgammon game

Board games

Shakespeare mentions two board games in his plays—tables (backgammon), which was played by the wealthy, and nine men's morris, which was played by poorer people.

Nine men's morris game

Summer celebrations

On May 1, people celebrated the arrival of summer by dancing around decorated poles called maypoles. In *A Midsummer Night's Dream*, Shakespeare writes: "They rose early to observe the rite of May."

Sports on Sunday

On Sundays, Englishmen practiced archery. The longbow, used in hunting, was also an important weapon in warfare.

Gentlemen shoot arrows at a target on the village green

Games and festivals

At quiet periods in the farming year, people found time for games and sports, such as cockfighting and soccer. There were also festivals to celebrate the changing seasons, religious events, and royal visits.

Entertaining royalty

The most exciting event in the countryside was a visit from Queen Elizabeth I. The local nobility spent vast sums of money on entertainments for the queen, such as this water show in 1591.

The lost years

We know little of what Shakespeare did from the time he left school, at the age of 15, until 1592, when he was described as an up-and-coming playwright in London. Church records show that in November 1582, Shakespeare married Anne Hathaway. He was 18, while Anne was 26 and expecting their first child, Susanna. In 1585, twins arrived, who were named Judith and Hamnet.

Telling tales
According to one story, Shakespeare had to flee Stratford after being caught poaching deer. This story comes from Shakespeare's first biography, written in 1709 by John Rowe.

A place in heaven
One in three babies died in the 1500s. Christenings were important so that babies would go to heaven if they died. Susanna was baptized in Stratford on May 26, 1583.

Hathaway's house
William's wife, Anne, grew up in a large farmhouse in the village of Shottery, just over 1 mile (2 km) west of Stratford. Today, the farmhouse is known as Anne Hathaway's Cottage.

Father's footsteps
In Shakespeare's day, sons often followed their fathers into the family business. William may well have helped his father in the family wool-dealing business.

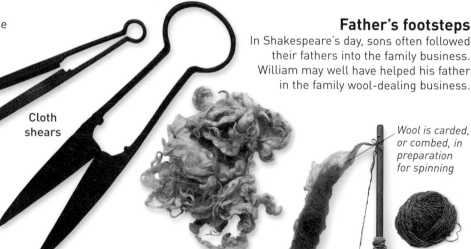

Cloth shears

Sheep shears

Unprepared sheep's wool

Wool is carded, or combed, in preparation for spinning

Spindle, used to spin wool into a thread

Ball of thread

Hunting for clues

For hundreds of years, scholars have hunted for clues that might explain what Shakespeare was doing during his "lost years." His writing shows knowledge of types of work such as medicine, soldiering, and the law, which suggests that he may have had some personal experience of them.

Coneys,
or rabbits

Wood
pigeons

Goose

In the army
In the 1800s,
scholar W. J. Thoms
found a document
naming a soldier
called William
Shakespeare.
But this man
was serving
in 1605, when
our Shakespeare
was a successful
playwright.

Medicine
Shakespeare's
work shows that
he had some
knowledge of
medicine, but
his characters
are often
scornful of
physicians,
or doctors.

Elizabethan plates
decorated with
paintings and
verses depicting
professions

Staging a slaughter
Writer John Aubrey claimed
that Shakespeare worked as a
butcher, adding that when William
killed a calf, "He would do it in a
high style, and make a speech."

*Spike to
make holes
for stitching*

*Half-
moon
shaped
blade*

*Hooked
leather
knife*

Leather-working tools

Green fingers
Shakespeare often
mentions gardening
activities, such as
weeding, in his plays.
This could mean that he
was a gardener for a time.

Case closed
Shakespeare's
plays are full
of legal terms.
In 1790, English
scholar Edmund
Malone suggested that
the playwright gained this
knowledge working in a legal office.

Leather working
Shakespeare is likely to
have learned leather-
working skills in his
father's workshop. He
would have used tools
like these to make
gloves, belts, or shoes.

16th-century engraving
of Richard Tarlton

Taking to the stage
In the 1580s, several acting companies
visited Stratford. England's leading
company, the Queen's Men, performed
in Stratford in 1587. William would
surely have seen the company, and
its star, Richard Tarlton. All we know
for certain is that, at some point,
Shakespeare became an actor.

Hand-colored engraving of
actors performing in an inn yard

Up to London

Apple-seller

In the 1580s, Shakespeare said goodbye to his family and set off to seek his fortune in London. He was just one of thousands of country people who moved to the great city in the late 16th century. On arriving, he would have been struck by the noise, dirt, and smells of the city. But he would have also been impressed by the beautiful churches and the grand mansions of the wealthy nobles.

A waterman was like a 16th-century taxi driver

Watermen worked either alone or in pairs

Crossing the river

Walking near the Thames River, Shakespeare would have heard the watermen calling out for passengers. The watermen rowed Londoners up and down the river, and across to Bankside and back.

A view of London from the south, by Dutch artist Claes Jans Visscher, c. 1616

Every day, thousands of people were rowed across the river to the playhouses at Bankside

Spreading city

When Shakespeare came to London, the city was spreading fast in all directions. Bankside, on the south bank, was rapidly becoming London's main entertainment center.

Merchant and his wife, 1590

"Sack! Sack!" shouts a man selling wine

"Pen and ink!" cries a man selling quills

"Trinkets and toys!" calls the tinker

"Almanacs!" cries a man selling books

"Mackerel!" shouts a fish seller

Sounds of the city

London was full of street sellers shouting out special cries to attract customers. Men and women wandered the streets, selling everything from vegetables, fish, wine, toys, and books, to quills and ink, fruit, brooms, pies, and secondhand clothes.

Merchants' might

The city was run by rich traders known as merchants. Trade was central to the wealth of the city, and every craft and trade had its own controlling organization, called a guild.

Building up

Staple Inn (right), where wool was weighed and taxed in Shakespeare's time, is still standing today. Since land was expensive, people built upward.

The Latin text along the top of the map describes London as "The most famous market in the entire world."

The bells of more than 100 churches rang out across the city

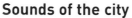

... TOTO ORBE CELEBERRIMUA

Shakespeare worshiped here, at St. Mary Overie's Church, later known as Southwark Cathedral

Set of 16th-century standard weights

Traitors' heads were displayed on poles on London Bridge to warn the public against committing treason

Measure for measure

The guilds controlled trade using standard weights. Official measurers would check that members were not cheating their customers.

London shows

Having grown up in sleepy Stratford, Shakespeare must have found London an exciting place. There was a variety of entertainments on offer. Londoners enjoyed watching cruel sports, such as bull or bear fights, and they often gathered to watch executions. Many enjoyed gambling at dice and cards, or playing sports, such as bowls.

Fighting chance
Cockfighting was a popular 17th-century sport. Onlookers would watch the birds fight to the death.

Rooster

Roosters fought with their beaks and spurred feet

Entertainment center
This map of London dates from 1572, just before the first playhouses were built. At this time, the only buildings for entertainment were cockfighting pits and bull- and bear-baiting houses.

LONDINVM FERA GLIAE REGNI

Londoners gather to watch an execution

Gory gallows
Watching executions for entertainment was a long-standing tradition. The executions of traitors were the most gruesome. The traitors were half-hanged, then their bellies were cut open and their inner organs burned in front of them.

Gallows were often built specially for each execution

Wooden gallows

Site of the Swan (built between 1595 and 1596)

Modern bulldog

Born to bite
At Bankside, Londoners could see bull-baiting with bulldogs that had been specially bred for the sport. The dog was trained to leap at the bull's face while the bull did its best to shake it off.

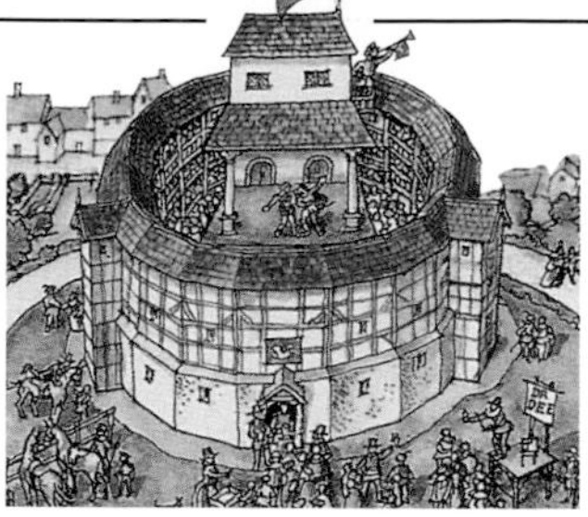

In it for the money

Most of the early theaters, such as the Swan and the Rose, were built by businessmen, who saw them as a way to make money. London's first playhouses were the Theatre (1576) and the Curtain (1577).

The Swan, built by Philip Henslowe, a dyer

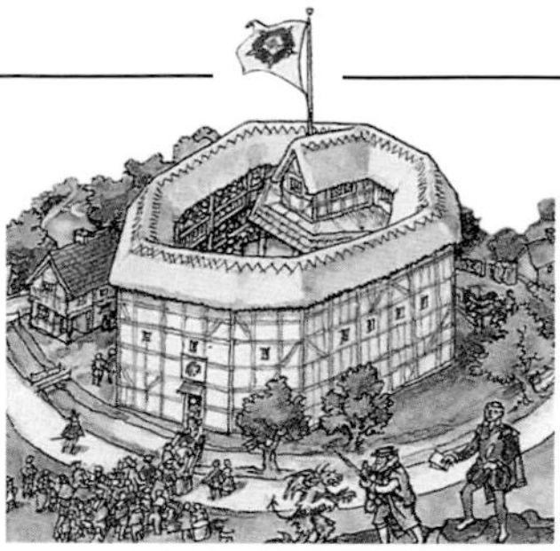

The Rose, built by Francis Langley, a goldsmith

Site of the Theatre

Site of the Curtain

Coneycatchers

London was full of criminals who made a living by cheating at cards and dice. The cheats were called coneycatchers, and their victims were known as coneys (rabbits).

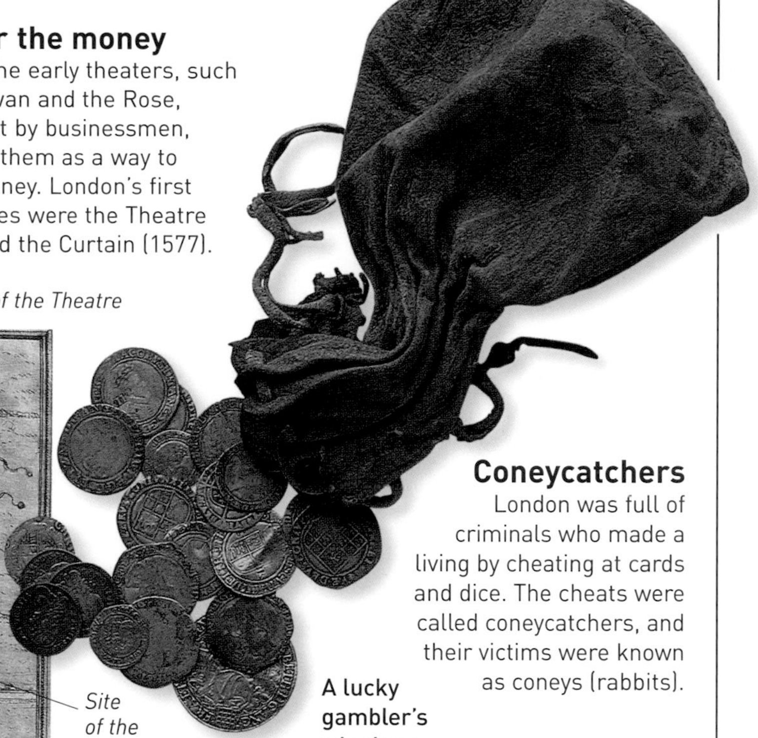

A lucky gambler's winnings

The bears had their own names, such as Harry Hunks

Brown bear

Bear Garden

Site of the Rose (built in 1587)

Bear-baiting in the 16th century

Tethered and toothless

In the Bear Garden, dogs were set against a bear tied to a stake. The bear's teeth were sometimes pulled out to give the dogs a better chance.

Queen Elizabeth I's court

When the Queen was not traveling the country, her court was based in the royal palaces around London. Elizabeth I surrounded herself with young male courtiers, who all competed for her favor. They flattered her by comparing her to the Roman moon goddess Diana, and called her "Gloriana," the glorious one.

Players at court
Elizabeth I never visited public playhouses. Instead, the players would perform private shows in the royal palaces. Shakespeare would have performed in front of the Queen before he became a playwright.

Pelican Queen
In this 1574 portrait, the 41-year-old Queen wears a pelican brooch. Female pelicans were thought to be perfect mothers, so the Queen wore this brooch to show how much she cared for her people.

White pearls symbolized the Queen's purity

Pelican brooch

Beauty secrets
The ladies at court used all kinds of lotions to try to remove spots or freckles. Herbs and spices were often used, but many of the recipes were harmful to health, or even poisonous.

Cloves

Ginger

Nutmeg

Bay

Spices and herbs were used in anti-freckle recipes

Opal

Drops from the deadly nightshade plant made the eyes sparkle

Mercury

Lemon

Lemon juice and poisonous mercury were used in face washes

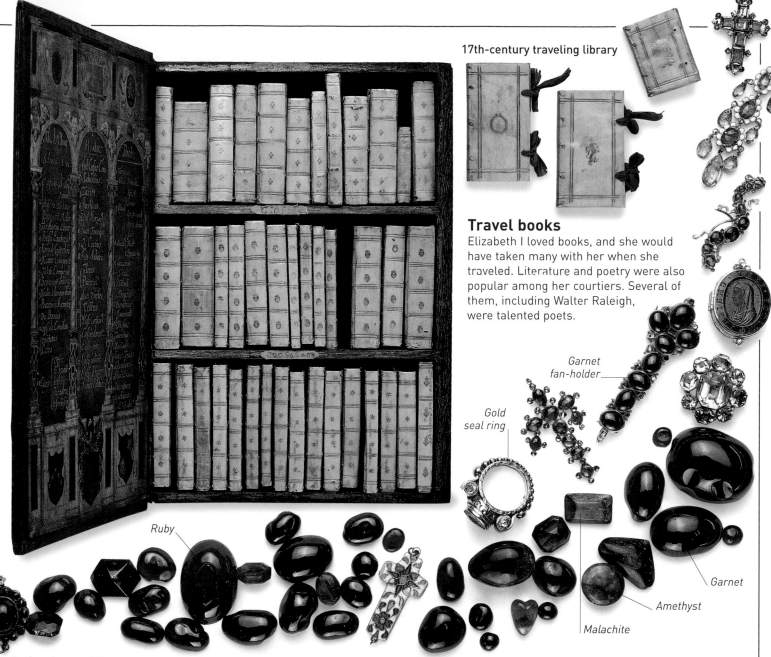

17th-century traveling library

Travel books
Elizabeth I loved books, and she would have taken many with her when she traveled. Literature and poetry were also popular among her courtiers. Several of them, including Walter Raleigh, were talented poets.

Garnet fan-holder

Gold seal ring

Ruby

Garnet

Amethyst

Malachite

Dripping with jewels
Both men and women at court competed to look as expensively dressed as possible. Courtiers spent lavishly on jewels, which they used to decorate every item of clothing from their shoes to their hats.

Signature of Elizabeth I

Pride comes before a fall
The Earl of Essex was one of the Queen's favorites. In 1601, he led a rebellion against the Queen, which failed, and Essex was beheaded. Shakespeare refers to the Earl's downfall in *Much Ado About Nothing*.

Signature of Robert Devereux, Earl of Essex

Royal procession
Elizabeth I's courtiers sometimes carried her through London in a seat called a palanquin. This gave ordinary people a chance to see their Queen. This 19th-century woodcut was copied from a 1601 painting by Robert Peake.

The playwrights

The London stage was dominated in the early 1590s by the plays of a group of university-educated men, such as Robert Greene, Christopher Marlowe, and Thomas Nashe. By 1592, Shakespeare was also an established playwright. His success was due partly to the fact that he was once a player—he knew what worked on stage and what did not.

Sweet revenge
Shakespeare learned to write by watching and acting in a new type of play called a "revenge tragedy," in which a murder is committed, then violently avenged. One of his first plays was the revenge tragedy *Titus Andronicus*.

The sloping surface allows the quill pen to be held at the right angle to the paper

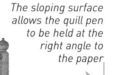

Making ink
Black ink was made from swellings called galls found on oak trees. The galls were crushed and mixed with water or vinegar and a chemical called green vitriol, made by pouring acid over rusty nails. The final ingredient was gum arabic, the dried sap of the acacia tree.

Oak leaf with gall

Rusty nails

17th-century inkwell and quills

Sitting comfortably
Before becoming a writer, the playwright Thomas Kyd worked as a scrivener, or copier of documents. He would have sat at a desk like this making neat copies of legal documents and plays. Most playwrights did not have special writing desks—they wrote wherever they could.

"Now, Faustus, let thine eyes with horror stare
Into that vast perpetual torture-house,
There are the furies tossing damned souls
On burning forks. Their bodies broil in lead."

CHRISTOPHER MARLOWE
EVIL ANGEL IN *DOCTOR FAUSTUS*

Tools of the trade

All educated people knew how to cut a pen from a goose feather using a penknife. Playwrights like Shakespeare had to keep their penknife close at hand, ready for when the quill's nib wore out and a new one needed to be cut.

The word pen comes from the Latin word penna, *meaning feather*

Last words

Just before his death in 1592, Robert Greene wrote an attack on Shakespeare, calling him an "upstart crow." He looked down on Shakespeare because he had not gone to university.

William Shakespeare's signature

Rapid writing

Writing seemed to come easily to William Shakespeare. His fellow playwright Ben Jonson wrote that "Whatsoever he penned, he never blotted out a line."

Carved penknives

Persian painting showing Timur on his throne

Dr. Faustus summons a devil using magic

Marlowe

The writer who most influenced Shakespeare was Christopher Marlowe (1564–1593). Marlowe put stirring speeches into the mouths of tragic heroes such as Dr. Faustus, a scholar who sells his soul to the devil.

Timur

Marlowe's first play *Tamburlaine* tells the story of Timur, a 14th-century Turkish warrior famous for his "conquering sword."

England at war

King of Spain
Philip II wanted to add England to his vast empire and bring the country back into the Catholic faith.

From 1585 to 1604, Protestant England was at war with Catholic Spain, ruled by King Philip II. The war created a mood of patriotism in the country, and people wanted to see plays drawn from English history with battles on the stage. So, in the 1590s, Shakespeare wrote nine plays dealing with English history, featuring kings, wars, and battles for the throne.

Spanish galleons were taller than English ships and harder to maneuver

God's winds
In 1588, a vast fleet of Spanish ships called the Armada was beaten in battle and scattered by storms. English people took this as a sign that God was on their side.

Henry IV comes to parliament to make his claim to the throne

Famous last words
The play *Richard II* tells how King Richard II was overthrown by his cousin, who became Henry IV. The play contains Shakespeare's famous patriotic speech, spoken by John of Gaunt: "This happy breed of men... this blessed plot, this earth, this realm, this England."

Sir John Falstaff
Falstaff is the drunken knight who befriends Prince Hal in the two *Henry IV* plays. The plays show a series of rebellions against Henry IV, whose troubled reign is God's punishment for overthrowing Richard II.

Agincourt
Henry V tells the story of England's great victory over the French at the Battle of Agincourt in 1415. "Follow your spirit," cries the King, "and cry God for Harry, England, and Saint George!"

Murder most foul
In *Richard III*, Shakespeare created one of his most famous villains. Richard murders his nephews in order to become king of England.

Linstocks from the wreck of the *Mary Rose*, which sank in 1545

Light my fire
Linstocks like these held lighted fuses for firing cannons on warships. By the 1580s, England had the most powerful warships in Europe. Real cannons were fired during the battle scenes in Shakespeare's history plays.

Pipe smoking was introduced to England from North America

Elizabethan pipes and smoking accessories

Model of a Spanish galleon

Each galleon bristled with cannons, which fired out through openings called ports in the sides of the ship

Tobacco pouch and pipe
This pouch and pipe belonged to Sir Walter Raleigh, the joint leader of a daring raid on the Spanish port of Cadiz in 1596. Raleigh also founded the first English settlement in North America.

Earl of Essex

Traitor
The other hero of the 1596 raid on Cadiz was the Earl of Essex. In later years, both Ralegh and Essex were beheaded as traitors.

27

Plague and poetry

Outbreaks of a terrible disease called the plague were common in Elizabethan London. Between 1592 and 1594, the plague was so bad that the playhouses had to stay closed for just over two years. There was no demand for Shakespeare to write new plays, so he turned to poetry instead.

Rats
People did not know it, but the plague was carried by fleas living on black rats. From 1592 to 1593, almost 12,000 Londoners died of the plague.

Black rat

Flea

The Earl of Southampton, painted by Nicholas Hilliard in about 1594

"Rich men trust not in wealth,
Gold cannot buy you health:
Physic himself must fade.
All things to end are made,
The plague full swift goes by;
I am sick, I must die:
Lord have mercy on us."

THOMAS NASHE
SUMMER'S LAST WILL AND TESTAMENT, 1592

Sage

Cautery

Marjoram

Lavender

Rosemary

Serious writing
During this time Shakespeare wrote two long poems, *Venus and Adonis* and *The Rape of Lucrece*, and dedicated them to his patron Henry Wriothesley, Earl of Southampton. Poets were more respected than playwrights, especially if they had aristocratic patrons.

Elizabethan golden pomander set with precious stones

Each section held a different herb

Hot rod
Doctors often used a hot metal rod called a cautery to burst the buboes (swellings) that appeared on plague victims. It was very painful and did little to help the patient.

Smelly city
Londoners thought that there was a link between the plague and the bad city air, so they tried to protect themselves by carrying pomanders (containers of sweet-smelling herbs).

A hat topped with ostrich feathers was the height of fashion

Clay pipes were introduced to England from the Americas in 1586

Scented streets

Rich women swung their jeweled pomanders in front of them, hoping that they would protect them from the plague. Rich gentlemen would fill the air around them with tobacco smoke.

The skeletons in this engraving symbolize the plague

Running away

In 1592, people started to flee London. Unfortunately, the plague followed them. By 1593, the disease had struck several other towns and cities in the country.

The pomander hung on a chain around the woman's waist

Strange cures

There was no cure for the plague, but pharmacists called apothecaries made medicines to sell. In *Romeo and Juliet*, Shakespeare describes an apothecary's shop full of strange things, such as "skins of ill-shaped fishes" and "musty seeds."

A gallant (fashionable man) with a noblewoman

Enemies and protectors

The popularity of the theater in London attracted hostility from powerful enemies. The Lord Mayor and his officials saw any large gathering as a threat to law and order, and were always trying to close down the playhouses. Fortunately, the actors were supported by the queen and her courtiers, who loved to watch plays.

Powerful patrons

In 1594, the Lord Chamberlain, Henry Carey (1524–96), became the patron of Shakespeare's theater company. Carey was the queen's cousin and one of her closest advisors.

Whipped out of town

It was against the law to perform plays without the permission of a powerful noble. Players caught performing illegally were whipped out of town.

The public was used to seeing criminals being punished in the streets

A beggar is whipped out of town

Scandalous!

In 1597, Ben Jonson was put in prison for writing *The Isle of Dogs*, a play said to be "full of scandalous matter." This shows that, despite their noble protectors, playwrights could still get into trouble if they put on controversial plays.

Portrait of Ben Jonson (1572–1637)

Lord Mayor

Aldermen, members of the council

Powerless protest

The Lord Mayor had no control over what went on outside the city walls, where most of the playhouses were built. All he could do was send letters of angry protest to the queen's ministers.

Puritans dressed more simply than other people

Puritans

The Puritans objected to the theater because they thought that people should spend all their time in work or prayer.

Some gentlemen were so busy applauding the players on stage that they did not notice they were being robbed

Lessons in lifting

London was full of thieves called cutpurses, many of whom worked in gangs. In 1585, a school for boy cutpurses was discovered in Billingsgate, London. The boys were taught how to steal coins from a purse without ringing the bells that were attached to it.

Cutting a purse was called "nipping a bung" in criminal slang

The cutpurse waits for the right moment to cut the purse strings

A gentleman's well-cut clothes stood out in the yard, where the poorest members of the audience gathered, and were likely to attract the attention of a cutpurse

Pants were worn tucked inside boots for riding

Boys made good cutpurses because they were small enough not to be noticed and had nimble fingers

Country gentleman

Visitors from outside London were less aware than city people of the risk of being robbed by a cutpurse. Robberies took place regularly in the playhouses. This provided the Lord Mayor with an argument for closing them, although he exaggerated the number of crimes committed.

Robbing place

Playhouses were ideal places for cutpurses because they were so crowded. Despite this, thieves were sometimes caught in the act and beaten up by angry members of the audience.

Jigs and jokes

Will Kemp was a popular comic actor in the Lord Chamberlain's Men. Kemp always danced a jig at the end of a show and in 1600, he danced from London to Norwich—a distance of more than 100 miles (160 km).

The players

In 1594, Shakespeare joined a new company called the Lord Chamberlain's Men. He wrote about two plays a year for them and also worked as an actor. The company performed at the Theatre in London, which was owned by James Burbage. Shakespeare invested money in the company and, in return, took a share of the profits.

Sly swordsman

William Sly was a player in the Lord Chamberlain's Men. He was a skilled swordsman and often played fiery young men like Hotspur in *Henry IV, Part One* and Tybalt in *Romeo and Juliet*.

Many costumes were made from scratch by members of the company

The stage hand sweeps up after a show at the Theatre

Hired help

The job of the stage hands was to fire the canon, make sure that props were in the right place, clear up the garbage, and operate the special effects.

Costumes and props were kept in baskets when not in use

Richard's rival

Edward Alleyn (1566–1626) was the star of the Lord Admiral's Men, and Richard Burbage's only real rival. He made his name playing Marlowe's heroes Dr. Faustus and Tamburlaine.

Tragic transformation

Shakespeare wrote his greatest tragic roles for James Burbage's son, Richard (1568–1619). Richard was famous for completely transforming himself into a character.

Dress, to be worn by a boy player playing a woman

Tireman admiring a new wig

Work table, where costumes were made and altered to suit new roles

Behind the scenes

This room in the modern Globe Theatre in London is designed to show visitors what a tiring, or dressing, room would have looked like in Shakespeare's day. Costumes, wigs, and props were all stored in the tiring room.

Costume care

The tireman was in charge of the costumes. Some of the costumes were bought from London tailors, while others were made by the company.

Building the Globe

In 1597, the Theatre was forced to close. It had been built on rented land and the lease had come to an end. In December 1598, the Burbage brothers hired workmen to pull the Theatre down. They took the oak beams by boat to Bankside, where they used them to build a new playhouse called the Globe.

The Globe's stage, as imagined by George Cruikshank in 1863

Round pegs and joints

Square pegs and joints

Knock down

The wooden joints of the Theatre were joined with pegs. The workmen could knock them apart with hammers and use the undamaged beams to make the new frame.

Wall story

After making the frame, the builders installed wall panels. These were made from wattle (woven mats of hazel stems) covered with daub (a mixture of clay, lime, straw, horsehair, and dung).

Interior decor

Special tools were used to carve and chisel the decorative features. The interior was colorful, with the stage columns painted to look like marble.

Awls for making small holes

Billhook for pruning and lopping

Auger for boring holes in wood

Hammer

Broad ax

Hand saw

Chisel

Gentlemen's room for wealthy spectators

Gallery seats

Hell (space beneath the stage)

Model theater

This model gives us an idea of how the Globe may have looked. It is based on a 1596 sketch of the Swan playhouse. Excavations in 1989 revealed that the Globe was 100 ft (30 m) wide.

Stamp showing the Globe (the theater actually had 20 sides)

Flying the flag

Each playhouse had its own flag, flown on the days of a performance. The Globe also had a sign above its entrance, showing Hercules carrying a globe.

The Rose

The Swan

The Globe

Pole for the playhouse flag

To tile or not to tile?

The roof of the Globe was made of layers of straw and reeds. Thatched roofs were far cheaper than tiled roofs, but they were also a fire risk.

Upper rooms, where cannons were fired as a sound effect

Thatched roof shielded the galleries from the weather

In a play, the balcony could represent castle battlements or an upper window

Heavens (stage roof)—the underside was painted to look like a starry sky

Two columns held up the heavens

Stage stuck out into the yard, where the poorest people stood to watch the plays

Staging a play

Plays at the Globe were performed in the afternoons, by daylight. The scenery was limited, but there were some wonderful special effects. Angels and gods were lowered from the "heavens," and devils and ghosts came up through a trapdoor on stage. At the back of the stage, there was a curtained-off area used for showing picturelike scenes, such as characters lying dead or asleep.

Swan stage
In 1596, a Dutch visitor named Johannes de Witt sketched the Swan playhouse, giving us the only image from that time of a Shakespearean stage. It is bare aside from a bench. The scene might be set anywhere, from a palace to a ship's deck.

Playing soldiers
When players rushed on stage in full armor, waving swords, the audience knew that they were watching a battle. If the players carried scaling ladders, as in *Henry V*, the battle would become a siege.

Platt from *The Seven Deadly Sins, Part Two*

Play plot
The "platt," or plot, of a play was posted backstage. It listed the scenes, with the exits and entrances of all the characters. The actors needed to refer to the platt because they had not read the whole play. Each player was given only his own part to learn.

"Our statues and our images of Gods... Our giants, monsters, furies, beasts and bugbears, Our helmets, shields, and vizors, hairs and beards, Our pasteboard marchpanes and our wooden pies..."

RICHARD BROME
LIST OF PLAYHOUSE PROPERTIES IN *THE ANTIPODES*

Morion, a type of Spanish helmet

Rapier was used for fencing

Dagger was used in the left hand

The belt had a scabbard, where the rapier was kept

Spilled blood
Pigs' or sheeps' blood was often used in scenes of violent death. In one play, a character had a fake head cut off. The head contained a pig's bladder, filled with blood, which gushed all over the stage.

Headless man
A "beheaded man" could be shown on stage using two actors and a special table. The audience would see the "headless" body of a man, with his head apparently displayed at his feet.

Grave trouble

The trapdoor allowed players to disappear and appear suddenly. The hole in the floor was also used to represent a grave. In this scene from a modern production of *Hamlet*, the trapdoor represents the grave of Ophelia.

Skull, a prop used in *Hamlet*

Useful props

Props helped to set the scene. Crowns were important props in the history plays. Skulls were used when actors were talking about death, and candles carried on to the stage told the audience that it was night.

Crown

Candle, often carried by a player dressed in a nightgown

The player puts his head through a hole in the table

Ruff was placed around the player's neck once his head was through the hole

The table surrounded by a curtain to hide what is underneath

The actor had to be careful not to blink or move

Music and dance

From the royal court to the peasant's cottage, music could be heard everywhere in Shakespeare's time. Many people played instruments, and Elizabethan audiences expected to hear good music when they went to the theater. In Shakespeare's plays, there are more than 300 stage directions calling for music. He also wrote more than 70 songs for his characters to sing.

A boy plays a viol to accompany a lively dance, late 1500s

A spring in your step

Many different dances were popular in Shakespeare's day. The galliard was a lively court dance with leaps, kicks, and springing steps, while the pavane was more stately. Ordinary people enjoyed less formal dances, such as the wild morris, danced with bells strapped to the legs.

Orpharian

This instrument was invented in 1580 by London instrument maker John Rose. He named it after Orpheus, a mythical ancient Greek musician.

Wire strings

Elaborately carved walnut body, inset with pearls and rubies

16th-century orpharian

Triangle

Lute

Couple dancing the galliard, by Flemish artist Hieronymus Francken the Elder, 1540–1610

Serenade in front of Silvia's window, by John Gilbert, c. 1860

Love song

In *The Two Gentlemen of Verona*, Thurio, who is in love with Silvia, hires musicians to "give some evening music to her ear." Music performed to win a woman's love is known as a serenade.

Sounds for clowns

The pipe and tabor (drum) were played at the same time by one person. They were used to accompany jigs—the clowns' dances at the end of a performance.

Pipe

Mysterious melodies

The hautboy, or shawm, made an eerie, solemn sound, which Shakespeare used to create an atmosphere of dread in his tragedies.

A woodwind instrument, like an oboe

Pipes produced a single continuous note called a drone

Hautboy

Second drone pipe

16th-century engraving by Crispin de Passe

Viol

Played with a bow, the viol was used to accompany dances. In *Twelfth Night*, the foolish Sir Andrew Aguecheek "plays o' the viol-de-gamboys" to appear fashionable.

Viol made in the 1600s

Mouthpiece

Lovers' lutes

A man often played the lute to win over the woman he loved. However, in *The Taming of the Shrew*, hot-tempered Katherina smashes Petruchio over the head with his lute!

Bagpipe blues

The bagpipe was mostly played at country dances. Falstaff, in *Henry IV, Part One*, says that he feels as sad as "the drone of a Lincolnshire bagpipe."

Bag was made of leather

The tune was played with the fingers on this pipe

Classic lute

The sheep's gut strings were plucked with the fingers and thumb

Bagpipe

"Let the sounds of music creep in our ears."

WILLIAM SHAKESPEARE
LORENZO IN
THE MERCHANT OF VENICE

Soothing sounds

Many people believed that soothing lute music had the ability to heal. In *King Lear*, the mad king is brought to his senses with music—almost certainly played on a lute.

Clothes and costumes

Players in Shakespeare's day always dressed in clothes of their own time. The wealthy paraded around in elaborate outfits that were padded to create startling shapes. There were strict laws about clothes, which were worn as a sign of rank. Players were the only people allowed to break these laws, when they dressed up as nobles on stage.

Leather and satin gloves

Sweet gloves
Fashionable ladies wore scented gloves. In *Much Ado About Nothing*, Hero says, "These gloves... are an excellent perfume."

17th-century diamond and amethyst necklace

Covered in jewels
Ladies covered themselves with items of jewelry and had diamonds and pearls sewn into their dresses and hair. The boy players wore cheaper costume jewelry made from glass.

Sleeves stuffed with bombast, or horsehair

Ruff made from lace

All puffed up
Rich women wore wide dresses with huge, padded sleeves. As a rule, the less practical the dress, the higher the rank of the wearer.

Portrait of Elizabeth Buxton by Robert Peake, c. 1589

Skirt held out by a farthingale frame

Fashions for the stage
Modern productions of Shakespeare's plays use clothes from many different periods of history. These 1920s designs for *As You Like It* are early 1500s in style. Other productions have been set in Victorian, Elizabethan, or modern times.

Elizabethan exaggeration

Under Elizabeth I, clothes worn by fashionable men called gallants grew even more exaggerated. Ruffs grew larger and padding became thicker. Legs were covered by trunk hose at the top, canions to below the knee, and nether stockings underneath.

Boy's hat

Gallant's hat

Hats off!

Men wore hats most of the time. Many gallants wore hats decorated with ostrich feathers, which they swept in front of them when bowing.

Linen ruff

A cartwheel ruff made the face look as if it were on a plate

Doublet with padded "peascod" belly

Trunk hose

Every gallant carried a sword

Canions

Nether stockings

A gallant of the 1590s, when smaller ruffs were back in fashion

A gallant of the 1580s, when ruffs were at their largest

Functional fashion

Less wealthy men wore cheaper fabrics such as wool instead of velvet or silk, and might have worn plain knee breeches rather than trunk hose and canions.

The right shoes

This carved horn was used by a gallant in the 1590s to help him slip on his shoes. It is engraved with the image of a man of fashion.

The boy player

In Shakespeare's time, only men could act on the English stage, so women's roles were performed by boys. Although these actors were called boy players, they probably played females until they were in their 20s. Shakespeare often had fun making the boy players act the parts of women disguised as men. For example, in the play *As You Like It*, the heroine Rosalind pretends to be a man named Ganymede.

The skirt is lowered over the farthingale

Woman in disguise

In the film *Shakespeare in Love*, Gwyneth Paltrow plays a woman who disguises herself as a boy because she wants to go on stage.

Tireman

Pulling the laces tight will give the boy a waist

4 Skirt over hoop
He puts on an embroidered skirt, which will show through the front of the dress.

Wheel, or French, farthingale

3 Outstanding!
The boy steps into a hooped farthingale that makes the skirt of the dress stand out.

2 Laced up
Next, he puts on a tight upper garment called a bodice. The tireman helps to lace up the back.

Fashionable figures
The fashion for exaggerated hips and rear ends was achieved with a farthingale—a series of hoops made of whalebone, wood, or wire—or a padded belt called a bum roll.

Bum roll

Wheel farthingale

Bell-shaped farthingale

The petticoat protects the skin from the stiff fabric of the rest of the costume

1 Getting started
The boy player is getting ready to play Rosalind, the heroine of *As You Like It*. He starts by putting on a petticoat.

The real thing

A boy player needed the help of the tireman to get ready for his performance. Once a boy was wearing his dress, makeup, and wig, he was totally convincing as a female. English travelers in Europe were always amazed to see real women acting there.

"If I were a woman I would kiss as many of you as had beards that pleased me."

WILLIAM SHAKESPEARE
ROSALIND IN *AS YOU LIKE IT*

Mortar and pestle

Lead

Tin

Talc

Green fig

Pasty pastes
There were various recipes for white makeup. One was a mixture of talc and tin that was burned in a furnace then ground up with green figs and vinegar. Another recipe used lead, a poisonous metal.

English roses
Pale skin was a sign of nobility, since people with tanned skin were likely to be laborers who worked outside. Rosy cheeks were also a sign of beauty. Boy players used the same type of makeup as noblewomen when they were on stage.

Rosy hue
The red pigment used on cheeks and lips was made by grinding a mineral called cinnabar, or by crushing the roots of the madder plant.

Cinnabar

Rosalind's dress is one of the most expensive costumes

Padded sleeves

Flat, stiff front called a stomacher

Luxurious, beaded satin fabric

A fluttering fan made a good prop for a boy playing a woman

5 Wearing heels
The dress is fitted over everything to complete the outfit, and the boy puts on a pair of heeled shoes. These are hidden by the dress, but wearing them will help him to walk in a ladylike manner.

6 Rosalind!
After putting on a ruff, wig, and makeup, the boy is ready to play Rosalind. He repeats the first line to himself: "Dear Celia, I show more mirth than I am mistress of."

The audience

Playgoing was a popular form of entertainment in the late 1500s. As many as 3,000 people would gather to watch a show. Farmers, sailors, and servants stood side by side in the crowded yard. Lawyers and merchants filled the gallery seats, while nobles sat in the gentlemen's rooms next to the stage.

In the gallery
In this early 1900s drawing of the Globe, the audience watches a performance of *Henry IV*.

The apple-wives found it hard to make a living if the playhouses were closed

Shakespearian snacks
Apples and pears were sold as snacks in the playhouses in Shakespeare's time. Different varieties were available at different times. The first apples to ripen were called "Juneaters" because they were ready for eating on June 29, St. John's Day.

Williams pears

Pippins, grown in orchards in Kent, were the most common variety of apple

Pippin apples

Apples were bought as gifts for noblewomen

Nut carpet
In 1988 and 1989, archeologists found hazelnut shells in the yards of the Rose and Globe. The shells were mixed with ash and used as a floor covering to keep the yards dry in wet weather.

Apple-wives
Female fruit-sellers called apple-wives loved the large audiences they found at the playhouses. They wandered around the yard and the galleries carrying baskets of fruit to sell to hungry customers.

According to the accounts of some theatergoers, groundlings stank of garlic and onions

Garlic cloves

The groundlings often heckled the players, shouting rude comments and throwing apples if they got bored

Money was carried in a purse dangling from a belt because few clothes at the time had pockets

Tankards were usually made from pewter or wood

Scarecrows
The people who stood in the yard were nicknamed "groundlings" or "scarecrows" because of their shabby appearance. They were also called "stinkards" because of the way they smelled.

Thieves
Playgoers risked being robbed by a cutpurse. Some thieves dressed as gentlemen and worked in the galleries, where the richest pickings were to be found.

Crowds of stinkards would sometimes start fights and riots—even the actors on the stage were not safe when they went on the rampage

Getting merry
Groundlings guzzled ale from tankards, while gallery folk preferred wine. Many of Shakespeare's characters, such as Sir John Falstaff in *The Merry Wives of Windsor*, drink a strong Spanish wine called sack.

"Your stinkard has the self-same liberty to be there in his tobacco fumes which your sweet courtier hath."

THOMAS DEKKER
THE GULL'S HORNBOOK, 1609

Comfort costs
It cost one penny to stand in the yard. For an extra penny, playgoers could sit in the gallery.

Coin found at the Rose playhouse

Shakespeare's comedies

In Shakespeare's time, a comedy meant a lighthearted play with a happy ending. In the 1590s, Shakespeare wrote 10 comedies, most of them with plots taken from old love stories. He liked stories in which young lovers overcome various obstacles before being allowed to marry. The lovers might have to put on a disguise or run away from home. But everything always turns out all right in the end.

Shylock

Portia

Pound of flesh
In *The Merchant of Venice*, Shylock, a money-lender, claims that Antonio owes him a pound of flesh for failing to repay a debt. Portia, the heroine, disguises herself as a lawyer to defend Antonio.

Forest of Arden
When Rosalind, the heroine of *As You Like It,* is banished from court, she goes to live in the Forest of Arden. Jaques, a miserable lord, is also banished to the forest, where he meets Touchstone, a jester who shares his upside-down view of the world.

Jaques   Touchstone

Love and marriage
Although people were fascinated by love stories, in real life they rarely married for love. The upper classes usually married for money, or to improve their social rank.

When the locket is closed, the lovers are face to face

16th-century locket containing miniatures painted by Nicholas Hilliard

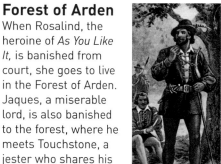

Valentine's day
Valentine, the hero of *The Two Gentlemen of Verona*, is exiled from Milan and captured by outlaws. The play ends with Valentine finding love and winning a pardon for his outlaw friends.

Ditched
In *The Merry Wives of Windsor*, Falstaff sends love letters to two "merry wives," hoping to get hold of their money. The wives find out and plot revenge. In one scene, Falstaff hides in a basket of dirty laundry and is then dumped in a ditch.

Magic and mischief
In *A Midsummer Night's Dream,* King Oberon asks Puck to drop a love potion in Queen Titania's eyes as she sleeps. On waking, she falls instantly in love with Bottom, the weaver. To cause mischief, Puck has given Bottom the head of a donkey.

Bottom, with the head of a donkey

Malvolio is usually stern and cold, so when he smiles continuously at Olivia she thinks that he has gone mad

Malvolio dreams of being made Count Malvolio

Oberon cures Titania with a herb, thought to be wormwood

Wormwood (*Artemesia absinthium*)

Malvolio's name means "bad will"

Malvolio's costume is usually made as farcical as possible for the scene with Olivia

MARY PICKFORD & DOUGLAS FAIRBANKS in ALL TALKING "TAMING OF THE SHREW" ALL LAUGHING
UNITED ARTISTS PICTURE

Making a good wife
This poster is for the 1929 film of *The Taming of the Shrew.* Petruchio, the hero, decides to marry bad-tempered Katherina for money, not love. The play shows how Petruchio goes about "taming" Katherina, turning her into an obedient wife.

Petruchio

Olivia has sworn to wear a veil for seven years, mourning her dead brother

Olivia

Crazy love
In *Twelfth Night,* Malvolio, the conceited steward of Olivia, receives a letter that he thinks is from Olivia. It says that she loves him, and tells him to wear yellow stockings and to smile at her. Malvolio follows the orders and ends up being locked up as a madman.

Malvolio, the central character of the comic subplot in *Twelfth Night*

"And each several chamber bless Through this palace with sweet peace; And the owner of it blessed Ever shall in safety rest."

WILLIAM SHAKESPEARE
OBERON IN *A MIDSUMMER NIGHT'S DREAM*

The King's Men

Queen Elizabeth I died on March 24, 1603, and the crown passed to her closest male relative, James VI of Scotland. He was crowned James I of England on July 25, 1603, founding the Stuart dynasty. James was a supporter of the theater, and became the patron of Shakespeare's company, which was renamed the King's Men. To please the king, Shakespeare wrote *Macbeth*, a tragedy with a Scottish setting.

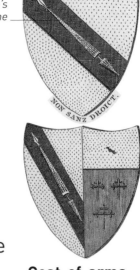

Spear from Shakespeare's name

Coat-of-arms
One sign of Shakespeare's growing success was that in 1596 he received a coat-of-arms, the badge of a gentleman.

James I of England
James I (1566–1625) was crowned in 1603, but was unable to come to London until March 15, 1604. He was kept away by a terrible new outbreak of the plague.

Royal touch
These gold "touchpieces" were given by James I to people suffering from a disease called scrofula. A royal touch was supposed to cure the disease.

Noble frog
In the early 1600s, it was fashionable for courtiers to carry purses in the shape of unusual objects or animals, such as this frog. Although frogs were linked with witchcraft in *Macbeth*, they were also a symbol of spring.

Macbeth cries, "Hence, horrible shadow!" when he sees Banquo's ghost

The ghost of Banquo makes a terrifying appearance at a feast

Crow

Toad

Evil spirits
Witches were thought to have evil spirit helpers, which took the shape of animals such as black cats, toads, and crows. In the 17th century, hundreds of innocent people were accused of witchcraft.

Black cat

Murder and treason
In *Macbeth*, the witches tell Macbeth that he will be king of Scotland, but that his friend Banquo will be the father of kings. Macbeth murders the king to seize the crown, then kills Banquo.

Curse of *Macbeth*

The black magic in *Macbeth* has led to a belief among superstitious actors that the play is cursed. According to the 17th-century writer John Aubrey, bad luck followed the play from its first performance, when the boy playing Lady Macbeth became sick and died. Actors try to beat the curse by never mentioning the play's title, calling it "the Scottish play" instead.

Actors say it is bad luck to wear costumes from Macbeth in any other production

This witch's costume was used in a Royal Shakespeare production of Macbeth

Achilles drags Hector's body behind his chariot

Hector's horrified parents watch from Troy

The dark colors of the costume reflect the description by Shakespeare of the ugly "midnight hags"

Dress made of torn strips of cotton

Comedy or tragedy?

This Roman lamp shows a scene from the Trojan war, the subject of Shakespeare's *Troilus and Cressida*, one of three plays that is difficult to categorize. *All's Well That Ends Well*, *Measure for Measure*, and *Troilus and Cressida* share many features of comedy, but they are also dark and gloomy in mood.

The famous tragedies

In the early 1600s, Shakespeare wrote the great tragedies *Hamlet*, *King Lear*, *Othello*, and *Macbeth*. These four plays contain Shakespeare's most famous poetry and provided his star Richard Burbage with his greatest roles. The plays also contain exciting action scenes, such as the fencing duel at the end of *Hamlet*.

Family feud

Romeo and Juliet tells the story of two young lovers who are kept apart by a family feud. It takes the tragic deaths of the lovers to bring the feud to an end.

Hamlet thrusts at Laertes's right shoulder, scoring a hit

Laertes tries to stab Hamlet, who deflects the blow

Laertes defends himself against Hamlet

Hamlet is the better swordsman

Laertes catches Hamlet off guard and cuts him with his poisoned sword—it will be his death blow

Hamlet thrusts at Laertes's thigh

Fighting fit

Players had to be skilled at swordfighting. Gentlemen learned fencing as part of their education, so if they saw clumsy fighting in a play they would boo the players off the stage.

Deadly duel

Hamlet does not know that the villain Claudius has persuaded Laertes to use a poisoned sword. In the duel, both Laertes and Hamlet are wounded by the sword. The dying Laertes confesses to Hamlet, who kills Claudius before he dies himself.

Street fight

Shakespeare wrote swordfights into several of his plays. In *Romeo and Juliet*, Romeo's friend Mercutio fights Juliet's cousin Tybalt in a street brawl.

OTHELLO

This poster, advertising a production of *Othello*, shows the Moor preparing to kill his sleeping wife Desdemona

Tricked

The hero of *Othello* is a Moor (North African) married to Desdemona. The evil villain, Iago, plots Othello's downfall by making him suspect that Desdemona is unfaithful. Driven mad by jealousy, Othello murders his innocent wife. Too late, he realizes that he has made a mistake.

Iago

Othello

Fencers used a light, thin stabbing sword called a rapier

Hamlet gazes at his father's ghost, but his mother Gertrude cannot see the ghost and thinks that her son is insane

Foolish father

In *King Lear*, an old king divides his kingdom between two wicked daughters and rejects the daughter who loves him. He eventually comes to understand how foolish he has been.

Most unnatural murder

In the 1947 film *Hamlet*, Laurence Olivier played the Danish prince. He is ordered by the ghost of his father to avenge his "foul and most unnatural murder."

Hamlet is the most complex of Shakespeare's heroes

Polonius, Laertes's father, is accidentally killed by Hamlet, who mistakes him for the king

*"So shall you hear
Of carnal, bloody,
and unnatural acts,
Of accidental judgements,
casual slaughters."*

WILLIAM SHAKESPEARE
HORATIO IN *HAMLET*

The Roman plays

In the early 1600s, both Shakespeare and Ben Jonson wrote tragedies set in ancient Rome. This subject was familiar to educated members of their audiences, thanks to the influence of Roman writers such as Seneca. Setting plays in Rome allowed playwrights to discuss political issues without risking offending the government.

Poster for a 1965 production of *Coriolanus*

Roman reject

In *Coriolanus*, Shakespeare tells the story of an ambitious Roman nobleman named Coriolanus, who is a great warrior but a poor politician. When the people of Rome reject Coriolanus, he joins the city's enemies, the Volscians.

Offending portrait

Julius Caesar (100–44 BCE) was the subject of Shakespeare's first Roman play. Caesar was a Roman general who was murdered because he started to act like a king. He was the first Roman to put his portrait on a coin, which offended many people.

Roman coin with the portrait of Julius Caesar

In the play Julius Caesar, *the ghost of the murdered leader returns to speak to Brutus, the man who killed him*

Brutus, who plans Caesar's murder

Mark Antony, who defeats Brutus in war

Brutus asks the ghost if he is "some devil that mak'st my blood turn cold and my hair to stare"

Murdering hero

The hero of *Julius Caesar* is Caesar's friend and killer, Brutus. After Caesar's murder, Mark Antony rouses the people of Rome with his famous speech, "Friends, Romans, countrymen, lend me your ears."

The folds of togas make good places for actors playing the killers in Julius Caesar to hide their daggers

Cobra, the type of snake with which Cleopatra may have killed herself

1940s US actress Katherine Cornell as Cleopatra

Cleopatra with her maid Charmian

Love before duty

In *Antony and Cleopatra*, Antony falls in love with Cleopatra, the Queen of Egypt. Lovestruck, Antony forgets his duties to Rome. The play ends with the suicide of the lovers. Antony stabs himself and Cleopatra makes a deadly snake bite her.

Togas or cloaks?

Roman citizens dressed in elaborately folded robes called togas. But Shakespeare would not have known what a toga was. The Roman characters in his plays would have worn cloaks, as courtiers did in Shakespeare's time.

In ancient Rome, purple was a sign of high rank

Squeaking Cleopatra

Miss Darragh played Cleopatra to Jerrold Robertshaw's Antony in this 20th-century production. Witty and clever, Cleopatra dies imagining her story being performed on stage, with a "squeaking" boy playing her role.

The romances

In 1608, the King's Men took over a second playhouse at Blackfriars. The new audience, made up of wealthy Londoners, inspired a new style of playwriting. Between 1608 and 1611, Shakespeare wrote four plays for the Blackfriars. Known as the romances, they have in common fairy-tale plots, the adventures of noble heroes and heroines, and families broken apart and reunited.

Regret and reunion
This photo is from a 1966 production of *A Winter's Tale*. King Leontes thinks that Polixenes is in love with his wife and locks her away. After she fakes her own death, the royal couple is reunited.

Shipwreck spell
The Tempest tells the story of Prospero, a magician living on an island with a band of fairy spirits. He uses magic to wreck a ship carrying his enemies.

Novel idea
Shakespeare was inspired by stories such as *Arcadia* by Sir Philip Sydney (1593). It tells the tale of two disguised princes in their search for love.

Stage romances
Shakespeare was also inspired by playwrights Francis Beaumont and John Fletcher, who had been writing stage romances since 1607. Fletcher later worked with Shakespeare on his last three plays.

Illustration for *The Tempest* by Robert Dudley, 1856

Prospero's spirits bring a banquet to the shipwrecked seafarers

Illustration for *Cymbeline* by Robert Dudley, 1856

*"... I come
To answer thy best
pleasure; be't to fly,
To swim, to dive
into the fire, to ride
On the curled clouds..."*

WILLIAM SHAKESPEARE
ARIEL IN *THE TEMPEST*

Plot twists
In the play *Cymbeline*, Posthumus and Imogen are forced to part when Posthumus is banished. *Cymbeline* has more plot twists than any other Shakespeare play, with eight surprises in a row in the final scene.

Chest holding Thaisa, found on the seashore

Miraculous music
Pericles tells the story of Thaisa, who is buried at sea by her grieving husband, Pericles. She is washed ashore at Ephesus, where she is brought back to life by the miraculous power of music.

Illustration from *The Children's Shakespeare* (1911) by Charles Folkard

Fancy dress
A type of court entertainment called a masque (a mixture of ballet, opera, and fancy costumes) influenced the staging at the Blackfriars playhouse. In *The Tempest*, Prospero stages his own masque with the help of magic.

The playwright's signature

Part of the legal document giving Shakespeare the rights to the house at Blackfriars

New house
In 1613, Shakespeare bought a house close to the Blackfriars playhouse. He did not spend much time there because he had already gone back to live in Stratford.

Woman in a masque costume, c. 1615

Sun and stars

The Sun and Moon are important astrological signs

"It is the stars, the stars above that govern our conditions," says the Earl of Kent in *King Lear*. In Shakespeare's time, many people believed in astrology—the idea that heavenly bodies could control or influence life on Earth. Elizabethan sailors also used the Sun and the stars to find their way at sea.

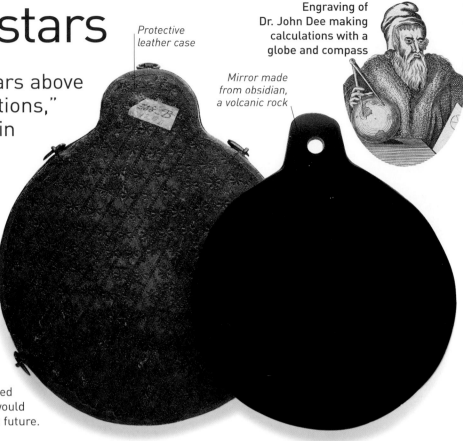

Protective leather case

Engraving of Dr. John Dee making calculations with a globe and compass

Mirror made from obsidian, a volcanic rock

Mirror, mirror
Royal astrologer Dr. John Dee (1527–1608) claimed he had received this mirror from an angel. He would gaze into the glass, hoping to see visions of the future.

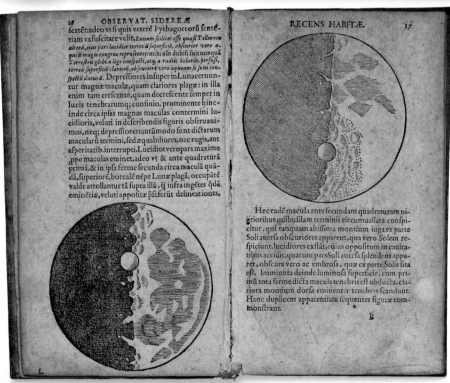

Galileo's 1610 book *The Starry Messenger*, showing the scientist's drawings of the cratered surface of the Moon

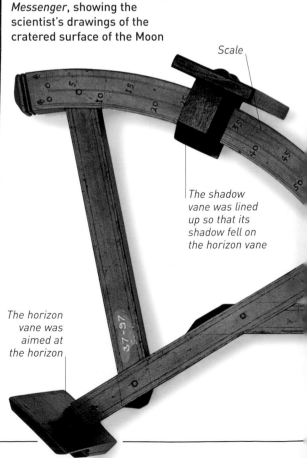

Scale

The shadow vane was lined up so that its shadow fell on the horizon vane

The horizon vane was aimed at the horizon

Star gazing
In 1609, Italian scientist Galileo Galilei (1564–1642) built a telescope to study the night sky. In 1610, he published his discoveries in a book called *The Starry Messenger*.

Well-equipped

Dr. John Dee was expert at navigating using the Sun and stars. His specialized equipment included a compass, a wind vane, and a sundial.

1625 engraving of an alchemist

The science of the stone

Dee was also interested in alchemy, the scientific search for the magical "philosopher's stone," which could turn metals such as lead into gold. Ben Jonson made fun of this practice in his 1611 comedy *The Alchemist*.

Sundial and compass

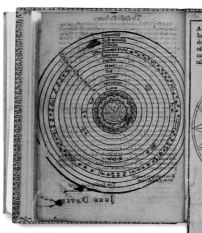

Table for calculating tides from the phases of the Moon

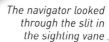

Wind vane

Wind vane screws into place here

Best book

In 1595, scientist John Davis (c. 1550–1605) wrote *The Seaman's Secrets*, the most accurate guide to navigation of the 16th century. Davis made three voyages into the Arctic, hoping to find a route to China.

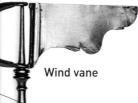

A replica of Galileo's telescope

Galileo's telescope was a great improvement on a Dutch invention

Backs to the Sun

John Davis also invented the back-staff, an instrument that determined a ship's latitude (north-south position) from the height of the Sun. With a back-staff, navigators could turn their backs to the Sun and use a shadow to measure its height.

Davis's back-staff, the most popular navigation instrument until well into the 17th century

The sighting vane was positioned at the estimated latitude

The navigator looked through the slit in the sighling vane

Secret studies

John Gielgud starred as scientist-magician Prospero in the 1991 film *Prospero's Books*, based on Shakespeare's *The Tempest*. Prospero describes himself in the play as being "rapt in secret studies."

"These late eclipses of the sun and moon portend no good to us."

WILLIAM SHAKESPEARE
THE EARL OF GLOUCESTER IN *KING LEAR*

Return to Stratford

After finishing *The Tempest* in 1611, Shakespeare returned to Stratford. Now a wealthy man, he went to live in New Place, the house that he had bought for his family in 1597. Shakespeare died on April 23, 1616, and was buried at the Holy Trinity Church in Stratford with the words "Curst be he that moves my bones" inscribed on his grave.

Home study

Shakespeare continued to write for about two years after he returned to Stratford. He visited London from time to time to work with John Fletcher on three plays *Henry VIII*, *Two Noble Kinsmen*, and a lost play called *Cardenio*.

Last lines

In 1613, Shakespeare wrote his last lines for the theater in the play *Two Noble Kinsmen*. This little-known play tells the story of two friends, Palamon and Arcite. The characters, shown here in a production of the play at the modern Globe Theatre, both fall for the beautiful Emilia, and rivalry in love turns them into bitter enemies.

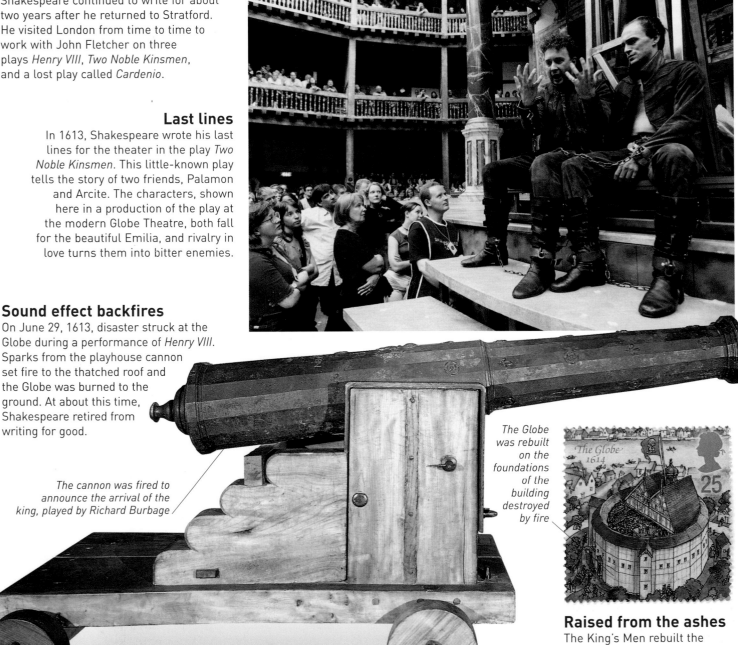

Sound effect backfires

On June 29, 1613, disaster struck at the Globe during a performance of *Henry VIII*. Sparks from the playhouse cannon set fire to the thatched roof and the Globe was burned to the ground. At about this time, Shakespeare retired from writing for good.

The cannon was fired to announce the arrival of the king, played by Richard Burbage

Elizabethan cannon with bronze barrel and reproduction wooden stand

The Globe was rebuilt on the foundations of the building destroyed by fire

The Globe 1614

25

Raised from the ashes

The King's Men rebuilt the Globe with a fireproof, tiled roof, and reopened it in 1614.

Hall Croft, Stratford

In 1607, Shakespeare's daughter Susanna went to live at Hall Croft with her new husband, John Hall. Shakespeare approved of John and would have returned home for the wedding. During his last years in London, Shakespeare would have returned to Stratford for events such as his mother's funeral in 1608.

A good likeness

In 1623, a stone statue of Shakespeare, sculpted by Geerart Janssen, was installed in the Holy Trinity Church. The monument is likely to be an accurate portrait of the writer, since it was approved by his family.

Will's will

Shakespeare left his houses and land to his eldest daughter, Susanna. His younger daughter Judith received £300, a large sum at the time. Shakespeare's wife Anne received only his second-best bed, but it is likely that she remained at New Place until her death in 1623.

Mourning jewelry was often decorated with reminders of death, such as skulls and skeletons

17th-century mourning ring

Remember me

Shakespeare also left money to his closest friends from the King's Men so that they could buy gold mourning rings in his memory.

Printed plays

17th-century image of a pressman laying out letters for printing

Shakespeare had little interest in seeing his plays in print. They were written to be performed and could reach a far larger audience at the Globe than they would as books. About half of Shakespeare's plays were published during his lifetime, as little books called quartos. Seven years after his death, Shakespeare's plays were published in a single volume, known as the First Folio.

Hard pressed
Printing in Shakespeare's day was a slow process. Metal letters in a frame were placed on a "coffin" and inked with a ball. A pressman put the paper on a frame called a tympan and lowered it onto the coffin. He then slid the coffin under a plate called a platen. Finally, he lowered the platen, pressing the paper onto the inky letters.

Heavy platen, or printing plate

Sturdy wooden frame

Hand press

Quarto
This edition of *A Midsummer Night's Dream* was printed in 1600. Each copy cost six pennies—six times the cost of seeing the play on stage. The name quarto, meaning fourth, comes from the fact that four pages were printed on each side of a single sheet.

First folio
In 1623, Henry Condell and John Heminges published 36 of Shakespeare's plays in the leather-bound First Folio. A folio (the Latin word for leaf) is a large book with pages made up of standard sheets, or leaves, of paper folded in half.

Illustrations of irises from John Gerard's *History of Plants* (1597)

Coloring in

Book illustrations were printed in black and white from carved blocks of wood. The color was added by hand, which was a slow and expensive process.

Printers usually worked in pairs

Bar to lower platen

Detail from a 17th-century engraving of a print shop

Leather ink ball, stuffed with horsehair

Sliding coffin

Shakespeare's coat-of-arms

Detail from an engraving of a pressman lifting a printed sheet

Tympan

Embroidered carrying bag for pocketbook

Book in a bag

It was fashionable to read pocket-sized books while walking in the open air. The books often contained short religious texts, to appeal to Puritans, or almanacs, which were predictions of the coming year's events.

16th-century pocketbook, with a gallant in a feathered hat for decoration

This book was designed to be displayed with identically bound editions of other Shakespeare plays

Unlimited editions

By 1913, when this copy of *Romeo and Juliet* was printed, hundreds of editions of Shakespeare's plays had been published around the world, reaching an audience far larger than Shakespeare could have imagined.

Shakespeare's legacy

"He was not of an age, but for all time," wrote the playwright Ben Jonson to describe his friend William Shakespeare, and he has been proved right. Shakespeare's plays are still performed all over the world and have inspired movies, ballets, musicals, and operas. His other great legacy is to the English language. Hundreds of everyday words and phrases such as "cold-blooded" and "fair play" appeared first in a Shakespeare play.

Dreamy dish
Designed in 1853 by W. B. Kirk, this porcelain fruit bowl is decorated with a lively scene from *A Midsummer Night's Dream*.

Herbert Beerbohm Tree as Cardinal Wolsey in *Henry VIII*

Captured in glass
This stained-glass window depicting some of Shakespeare's comic characters is in Southwark Cathedral, London, where the playwright worshiped. The window, designed by Christopher Webb, was unveiled in 1954.

Cartoons
In the 1990s, some of Shakespeare's plays were made into cartoons for children's television. In this scene from *A Midsummer Night's Dream*, Oberon is about to wake Titania from a spell, saying, "Now my Titania; wake you, my sweet queen."

Spectacular Shakespeare
British actor-manager Herbert Beerbohm Tree was famous for his spectacular and lavish productions of Shakespeare's plays in the late 19th and early 20th centuries.

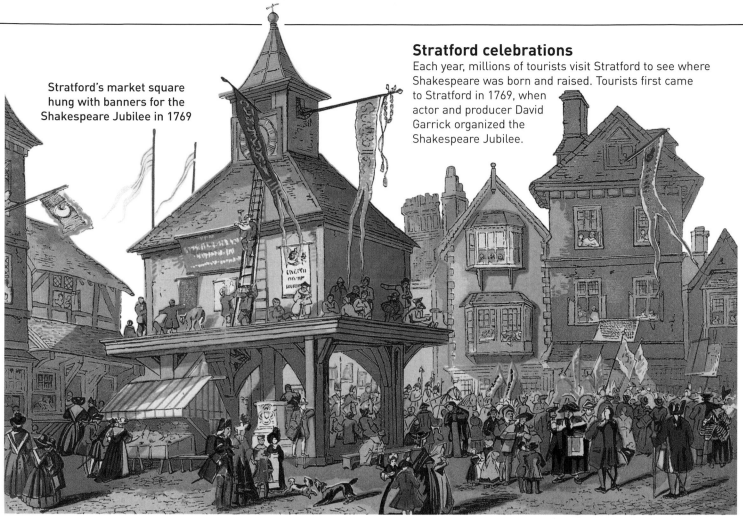

Stratford's market square hung with banners for the Shakespeare Jubilee in 1769

Stratford celebrations

Each year, millions of tourists visit Stratford to see where Shakespeare was born and raised. Tourists first came to Stratford in 1769, when actor and producer David Garrick organized the Shakespeare Jubilee.

Putting it to music

In the 1940s and '50s, two of Shakespeare's plays were turned into popular musicals—*Kiss Me Kate*, based on *The Taming of the Shrew*, and *West Side Story*, which is the tale of *Romeo and Juliet* set in New York. Operatic adaptations of Shakespeare's plays include Verdi's *Macbeth*, *Othello*, and *Falstaff*, all composed in the second half of the 19th century.

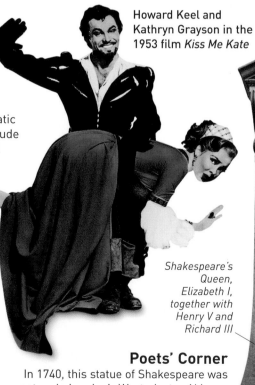

Howard Keel and Kathryn Grayson in the 1953 film *Kiss Me Kate*

Shakespeare's Queen, Elizabeth I, together with Henry V and Richard III

Tempest in space

The 1956 film *Forbidden Planet* takes the story of Shakespeare's play *The Tempest* and sets it in outer space.

Poets' Corner

In 1740, this statue of Shakespeare was set up in London's Westminster Abbey. It overlooks Poets' Corner, where some of Britain's greatest poets are buried or have memorials.

Did you know?

SHAKESPEARE TIMELINE

Elizabeth I ruled England for 45 years

1558
Elizabeth, daughter of Henry VIII and Anne Boleyn, is crowned queen.

1564
William Shakespeare is born in Stratford-upon-Avon, England.

1568
The actor Richard Burbage is born.

1582
Shakespeare is married to a local farmer's daughter, Anne Hathaway.

1583
Shakespeare's first child, his daughter Susanna, is born.

Shakespeare's birthplace

1585
Shakespeare's wife gives birth to twins, Judith and Hamnet.

c. 1587
Shakespeare leaves his family in Stratford to establish himself in London as an actor and playwright.

1588
The English naval fleet defeats the invading Spanish Armada of nearly 150 ships, sent by Philip II, king of Spain. This was one of the more dramatic episodes in England's bitter war with Spain, which lasted from 1585–1604.

1591
Shakespeare begins to court the patronage of the royal family and dedicates his poem *Venus and Adonis* to Henry Wriothesley, the Earl of Southampton.

1592
The plague sweeps through London, causing many of the city's playhouses to close for the next two years.

1594
Shakespeare becomes a founding member of the acting group the Lord Chamberlain's Men. The company performs at the Theatre in north London. Over the next two years, he begins to gain recognition as the leading playwright in London.

1596
Shakespeare's son Hamnet dies at age 11. Shakespeare's father, John, reapplies successfully for a family coat-of-arms.

1597–1598
Shakespeare purchases the New Place residence in Stratford-upon-Avon.

1599
The Globe is built in Bankside, London, from the beams of the old Theatre.

Cannonball used by English fleet

1601
Shakespeare's father dies.

1603
James VI of Scotland becomes James I of England. The plague sweeps through London once again. The Lord Chamberlain's Men become the King's Men, the favorite acting company at court.

1607
Shakespeare's daughter Susanna marries Dr. John Hall.

1608
The King's Men begin to play at Blackfriars. Shakespeare's mother dies.

1609
The *Sonnets* are published.

1612
During the next few years, Shakespeare gradually moves back to Stratford. He buys a house in Blackfriars in 1613, but does not spend much time there.

Rossetti painting of *Henry IV, Part One*

1613
The Globe Theatre is burned down when the thatched roof catches fire.

1616
Shakespeare's daughter Judith marries Thomas Quiney. Shakespeare revises his will. A month later, on April 23, he dies and is buried at the Holy Trinity Church in Stratford.

1623
Shakespeare's First Folio is published by his fellow actors. It contains 36 of his plays.

Shakespeare memorial in Hyde Park, London

THE PLAYS OF SHAKESPEARE

HISTORIES
Henry VI, Part One (c. 1589–92)
Henry VI, Part Two (c. 1589–92)
Henry VI, Part Three (c. 1589–92)
Richard III (1592)
Richard II (1595)
King John (1596)
Henry IV, Part One (1597)
Henry IV, Part Two (1598)
Henry V (1599)
Henry VIII (1613)

TRAGEDIES
Titus Andronicus (1592–93)
Romeo and Juliet (1595)
Julius Caesar (1599)
Hamlet (1601)
Troilus and Cressida (1602)
Othello (1604)
King Lear (1605)
Macbeth (1605)
Antony and Cleopatra (1606)
Timon of Athens (1606)
Coriolanus (1608)

COMEDIES
The Comedy of Errors (1590)
The Taming of the Shrew (1591)
Love's Labour's Lost (1593)
The Two Gentlemen of Verona (1593)
A Midsummer Night's Dream (1594)
The Merchant of Venice (1596)

The opening scene of *The Tempest* is a mighty shipwreck caused by Prospero

The Merry Wives of Windsor (1597)
As You Like It (1599)
Much Ado About Nothing (1599)
Twelfth Night (1600)
All's Well That Ends Well (1603)

Measure for Measure (1604)
Pericles, Prince of Tyre (1607)
Cymbeline (1609)
A Winter's Tale (1610)
The Tempest (1611)

AMAZING FACTS

Shakespeare invented the word "assassination," among others.

The Bard wrote an average of 1.5 plays per year from 1589–1613.

Cardenio, a play thought to have been written by Shakespeare and performed during his lifetime, has been lost to history.

Shakespeare willed his fortune to his eldest daughter, and only a bed to his wife.

There have been more than 500 film and TV adaptations of Shakespeare's dramas.

Hamlet movie poster from 1948

QUERIES

Q What is the mystery surrounding Shakespeare's *Sonnets*?

A Shakespeare wrote 154 poems called sonnets. Some are addressed to an unidentified young nobleman; others speak of a "dark lady." Some people even query whether Shakespeare was the author of the poems. When the *Sonnets* were published in 1609, they were addressed to "Mr. W. H." This gave rise to the theory that the young man was Henry Wriothesley, Shakespeare's patron.

Q How many works did Shakespeare author?

A As with all aspects of Shakespeare's life, the facts are not clear. The 36 plays published in the First Folio are mostly agreed upon. *Pericles* was published later, as was *The Two Noble Kinsmen*, which Shakespeare is believed to have contributed to. Including the controversial lost *Cardenio*, this brings the potential total number of plays to 39. Shakespeare also wrote many poems, including 154 sonnets, *Venus and Adonis*, and *The Rape of Lucrece*.

Henry Wriothesley, Earl of Southampton

Who's who?

Here we examine some of Shakespeare's best-known characters. The plays in which they appear are noted at the end of each profile.

HEROES

Shakespeare's most famous heroes appear in the tragedies. These men are often noble, but have a character flaw that leads to their downfall.

Brutus
Brutus is a man of noble principles. Although he leads a plot to kill his friend, Julius Caesar, it is only for the good of the Roman state. He kills himself when he loses the war with Caesar's avengers. (*Julius Caesar*)

Coriolanus
Coriolanus is a brave Roman general whose arrogance makes the people of Rome reject him. He joins Rome's enemies and leads them against his own city. Finally, he agrees to spare Rome although he knows he will be killed. (*Coriolanus*)

Hamlet
Hamlet is Shakespeare's most complex character. His father, the king of Denmark, has been murdered by his brother for the throne. Hamlet's tragedy is that he is unsuited to the role of avenger, which is forced on him by his father's ghost. (*Hamlet*)

King Lear
King Lear's flaws are vanity, a lack of awareness, and an uncontrollable temper. He fails to see which of his daughters truly loves him, sending him on a path to madness. (*King Lear*)

Macbeth
After a witches' prophecy, Macbeth murders the king to take the crown. His ambition transforms him from a loyal soldier into a monster. (*Macbeth*)

Laurence Fishburne plays Othello in the 1995 film adaptation

Othello
Othello's vulnerability stems from his position as an outsider (he is a Moor from northern Africa) in sophisticated Venice. He is easily manipulated by evil Iago into believing that his wife has been unfaithful, and he kills her in a fit of jealousy. When Othello finds out that his wife was innocent, he commits suicide. (*Othello*)

HEROINES

Miranda in *The Tempest*

Shakespeare's women can be tragic or comic. They often cross-dress as men to gain more freedom.

Beatrice
After quarreling with Benedict, witty Beatrice ultimately falls in love with him. (*Much Ado About Nothing*)

Desdemona
The honest, loving, and naive wife of Othello is unjustly murdered by her suspicious husband. (*Othello*)

Hermione
The wife of a jealous king who accuses her of adultery when she is pregnant. (*A Winter's Tale*)

Isabella
A brave and clever nun who leaves her calling to help her brother Claudio. (*Measure for Measure*)

Katherina
The feisty bride of Petruchio, who teaches her how to be an obedient wife. (*The Taming of the Shrew*)

Miranda
Miranda grows up on an enchanted island where she falls in love with a shipwrecked prince. (*The Tempest*)

Ophelia
A fragile young woman who is rejected by Hamlet. Driven insane, she drowns herself. (*Hamlet*)

Portia
Strong and intelligent Portia disguises herself as a lawyer to save the man she loves. (*The Merchant of Venice*)

Viola
Viola disguises herself as a man and works for a count with whom she falls in love. (*Twelfth Night*)

LOVERS

Shakespeare's love stories are full of passion and tragedy.

Antony and Cleopatra
Mark Antony neglects his political duties in Rome to spend time with Cleopatra, the beautiful queen of Egypt. When he returns to Rome, he is persuaded to marry Caesar's sister, Octavia. In the ensuing betrayal and treachery, both lovers commit suicide. (*Antony and Cleopatra*)

Romeo and Juliet
Two teenagers from rival families in Verona marry in secret, and Juliet fakes her own death to escape her family's plans to marry her off to another man. In a misunderstanding, however, Romeo believes his wife to be truly dead and kills himself. When Juliet discovers his body, she too commits suicide. (*Romeo and Juliet*)

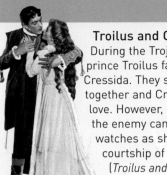

Troilus and Cressida
During the Trojan war, young prince Troilus falls in love with Cressida. They spend one night together and Cressida swears her love. However, she is then sent to the enemy camp where Troilus watches as she accepts the courtship of Diomedes. (*Troilus and Cressida*)

Painting of actors playing Romeo and Juliet

VILLAINS

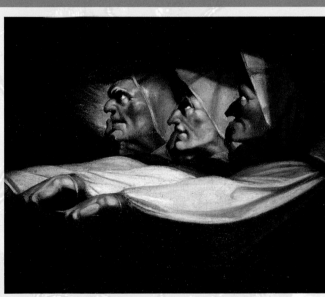

The three witches cause the downfall of Macbeth

Shakespeare's most exciting characters are often his villains.

Aaron
The servant to and lover of the queen of the Goths orders a violent attack on Titus Andronicus's daughter, Lavinia. (*Titus Andronicus*)

Edmund
Edmund plots to destroy his trusting brother and father to become Duke of Gloucester. (*King Lear*)

Iago
Wicked Iago delights in deceiving Othello into believing that his wife is unfaithful. (*Othello*)

Richard III
A ruthlessly ambitious duke who orders the murder of his brother and two innocent nephews to become king. (*Richard III*)

Shylock
Shylock is both villain and victim. However, his demand that Antonio give him a pound of flesh for an unpaid debt is morally evil. (*The Merchant of Venice*)

Three witches
Three "black and midnight hags" plot evil against Macbeth using prophecies and spells. (*Macbeth*)

FOOLS

These characters not only provide humor, but often wise words as well.

Bottom
Bottom the weaver ends up with the head of a donkey after a practical joke. (*A Midsummer Night's Dream*)

Dogberry
The ridiculous constable in charge of the night watch misuses words to comic effect. (*Much Ado About Nothing*)

Falstaff
This pleasure-loving coward appears in several plays. (*Henry IV, Parts 1 and 2; The Merry Wives of Windsor*)

Feste
A court jester, who makes his living by making others laugh. (*Twelfth Night*)

Fool
Known simply as Fool, this wise court jester often tells King Lear uncomfortable truths. (*King Lear*)

Nurse
Juliet's companion often talks nonsense, but is also a likeable character. (*Romeo and Juliet*)

Touchstone
The court fool who utters cynical truths. (*As You Like It*)

A court jester wore a cap and bells

Find out more

There are many ways you can find out more about Shakespeare's life and works. Many libraries hold videos of stage performances or film adaptations. You could also visit Stratford-upon-Avon or the reconstructed Globe Theatre in London.

The Great Hall in the Folger Shakespeare Library

Festivals

Theater communities often celebrate the work of Shakespeare with a festival in his honor. This production of *The Merchant of Venice* was part of a Shakespeare festival held in Canada.

Educational resources

Most public libraries have a lending section dedicated to the works of Shakespeare. The Folger Library in Washington, D.C., holds thousands of rare editions of Shakespeare's works in hundreds of different languages.

USEFUL WEBSITES

- Discover the history of the Bard's hometown:
  www.stratford-upon-avon.co.uk
- Great resource guide with history, timeline, quotations, and essays on all things Shakespeare:
  www.absoluteshakespeare.com
- Photographs and videos of the Royal Shakespeare Company productions:
  www.rsc.org.uk/explore
- The complete works of the Bard online:
  www.bartleby.com/70/

Water reed from Norfolk was used to thatch the roof of the new Globe

The gates show the flora and fauna of Shakespeare, and each creature or plant illustrates a line from a play

The Globe

The Globe Theatre in London was built as a replica of Shakespeare's original Globe Theatre. The theater is an open-air playhouse and the season runs from May to September, when the weather is good.

Stratford-upon-Avon

During a visit to Shakespeare's hometown, you can view the house in which he was born, the school he attended, his burial place, and Anne Hathaway's cottage. You can also see productions of his plays at Stratford's fine theaters, such as the Royal Shakespeare Theatre (above).

STRATFORD BOYS' GRAMMAR SCHOOL, STRATFORD-UPON-AVON, ENGLAND
The King Edward VI Grammar School in Stratford-upon-Avon dates back to the 13th century and still has more than 400 pupils today. Shakespeare would have attended the school for several years from about the age of seven.

Pupils at Stratford Boys' Grammar School in the 1960s

THE UNDERGLOBE, GLOBE THEATRE, LONDON
Underneath the Globe Theatre is a vast exhibition space dedicated to the historical era in which Shakespeare lived.

THE TOWER OF LONDON, ENGLAND
Visit the Bell Tower, where Elizabeth I locked up her enemies and was herself once a prisoner.

THE HOLY TRINITY CHURCH, STRATFORD-UPON-AVON, ENGLAND
Built in 1210 on the banks of the Avon River, the Holy Trinity Church is Stratford's oldest surviving building. It is at this church that Shakespeare was baptized and buried.

Every detail reflects the number three, for the Holy Trinity

An Elizabethan triangular lodge in Northamptonshire, England

Romeo declares his love for Juliet with the gift of a rose

School production of *Romeo and Juliet*

Elizabethan history

Discover more about Shakespeare by investigating the age in which he lived. Visit your local library to find information on the Elizabethan era. Do research online and study surviving Elizabethan architecture, which was amazingly intricate.

School plays

One of the best ways to understand the plays of Shakespeare is to act one out. If performing on stage is not for you, get together with friends and choose your favorite scenes and read them aloud.

Glossary

ALDERMAN A senior official in a local council.

ARCHERY A popular Elizabethan sport in which a bow is used to shoot an arrow at a target.

ARMADA A fleet of ships sent by Philip II of Spain to invade England in 1588.

BLOODSPORT Public entertainment during the Elizabethan era in which crowds watched cruel fights between dogs, bears, and other animals.

CATHOLIC A branch of Christianity that traditionally descends from the original church before the division with Protestantism occurred.

CONEYCATCHERS Professional cheats who made money from gambling. Coney was a slang term for "rabbit."å

COURT The residence of the monarch, in which the king or queen ruled over affairs of the state and also received visitors and enjoyed entertainment.

CRUCIFIX A cross or image of a cross representing Christ's crucifixion.

DUEL A prearranged and supervised fight with weapons between two individuals as a means of settling a dispute.

Mr. WILLIAM
SHAKESPEARES
COMEDIES,
HISTORIES, &
TRAGEDIES.
Published according to the True Originall Copies.

LONDON
Printed by Isaac Iaggard, and Ed. Blount. 1623.

First Folio

EXECUTION The killing of a criminal proven guilty by the state. In the Elizabethan era, criminals were often hanged on the gallows.

FIRST FOLIO The first edition of Shakespeare's collected works, which was published in 1623 and contained 36 plays.

FOLIO A sheet of paper folded in half to make four pages of a book.

GALLANT A fashionably dressed gentleman.

GALLOWS A wooden structure with a horizontal beam that holds a rope for hanging criminals.

HORNBOOK A page with text held in a frame with a thin window of flattened cattlehorn over it. These were widely used by pupils in school before books were commonplace.

IAMBIC PENTAMETER A type of verse used in plays and sonnets in the 16th and 17th centuries. Each line has 10 syllables with five stresses.

INKWELL A pot for holding ink and into which a quill was dipped for writing.

LUTE A stringed musical instrument.

MACE A ceremonial staff carried by certain officials, such as a mayor or a monarch.

MERCHANT A business person who trades goods or services, especially on the international market.

NIB The pointed tip of a quill, which was dipped in ink and used for writing.

PALANQUIN A luxurious covered seat or bed, carried on the shoulders of at least four men. Palanquins were used to transport important people such as royalty in public.

PATRIOTISM Love for and loyalty to one's country.

Rope for hanging

Wooden gallows

PENDANT A piece of jewelry hung on a chain around the neck.

PLAGUE A contagious and fatal disease that killed millions in England. It was spread by fleas living on black rats.

PLAYWRIGHT A writer of stage drama.

PROTESTANT A branch of Christianity set up in "protest" against Catholicism during the 15th century.

PURITAN Puritans were extremely strict Protestants who wanted to rid their church of all traces of Catholicism. Puritans led a very simple lifestyle, and they considered any pleasure to be bad.

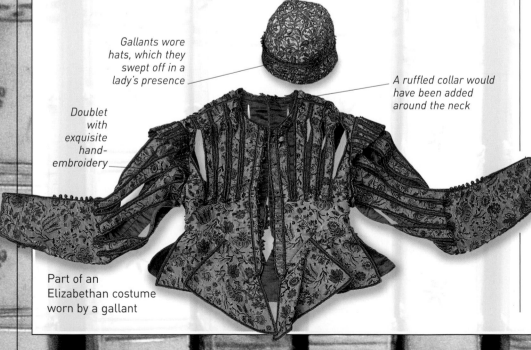

Gallants wore hats, which they swept off in a lady's presence

A ruffled collar would have been added around the neck

Doublet with exquisite hand-embroidery

Part of an Elizabethan costume worn by a gallant

QUARTO
A sheet of paper folded into quarters to make eight pages of a book.

An orpharian, a type of lute

QUILL A large, stiff feather from the tail or wing of a bird, used for writing.

REVENGE TRAGEDY A tragic drama in which the hero seeks revenge for a wrong done, often the murder of a relative.

ROMANCE A term sometimes used to describe four of Shakespeare's plays: *Cymbeline*, *Pericles*, *The Tempest*, and *A Winter's Tale*, which share fairy-tale plots and the theme of great families divided and reunited.

ROSARY BEADS A Roman Catholic prayer tool. The beads were used to help count the number of prayers being said.

RUFF A frilly collar worn by fashionable noblemen, made from starched linen.

SCRIVENER A professional writer who made a living from copying books by hand in the days before mechanical printing.

SERENADE A piece of evening music, often played outside the house of a woman to win her love.

TAPESTRY A woven, ornamental fabric, often used for wall hangings or furnishings.

Elizabethan pendant

TRAGEDY A type of drama that originated in classical Greece. A tragedy typically centers on a great hero who falls from power due to a combination of his personal failings and difficult circumstances.

TRAITOR A person who is guilty of betraying their country, their monarch, or a friend.

TREASON Betrayal of one's ruler.

TRUNDLE BED A low bed on wheels stored under a larger bed.

VERSE Poetry, or a division of a poem.

VESTMENT A special robe worn by clergy for religious ceremonies.

Selection of feather quills

Quotations

Here are some of the most memorable lines from Shakespeare's plays.

HUMAN NATURE
In nature there's no blemish but the mind; none can be called deform'd but the unkind—Antonio
(*Twelfth Night*, Act iii, scene 4)

Wisely and slow; they stumble who run fast—Friar Laurence
(*Romeo and Juliet*, Act ii, scene 3)

Have more than thou showest; speak less than thou knowest; lend less than thou owest—Fool (*King Lear*, Act i, scene 4)

DEATH
All that lives must die, passing through nature to eternity—Hamlet
(*Hamlet*, Act i, scene 2)

TRUTH
To thine own self be true, and it must follow, as the night the day, thou cannot then be false to any man—Polonius (*Hamlet*, Act i, scene 3)

It's not enough to speak, but to speak true—Lysander (*A Midsummer Night's Dream*, Act v, scene 1)

LIFE
To be, or not to be: that is the question—Hamlet (*Hamlet*, Act iii, scene 1)

All the world's a stage; and all the men and women merely players—Jaques (*As You Like It*, Act ii, scene 7)

There is nothing either good or bad, but thinking makes it so—Hamlet (*Hamlet*, Act ii, scene 2)

REPUTATION
Friends, Romans, countrymen, lend me your ears; I come to bury Caesar, not to praise him. The evil that men do lives after them—Mark Antony (*Julius Caesar*, Act iii, scene 2)

Hamlet ponders life and death

SPELLS
Double, double toil and trouble; fire burn and cauldron bubble—Three witches (*Macbeth*, Act iv, scene 1)

TIME
Come what come may; time and the hour runs through the roughest day—Macbeth (*Macbeth*, Act i, scene 3)

FRIENDSHIP
I am not of that feather, to shake off my friend when he must need me—Timon (*Timon of Athens*, Act i, scene 1)

They that thrive well take counsel of their friends
(*Venus and Adonis*)

Love all, trust a few, do wrong to none—Countess Rossillion (*All's Well That Ends Well*, Act i, scene 1)

LOVE
The course of true love never did run smooth—Lysander (*A Midsummer Night's Dream*, Act i, scene 1)

Love comforteth like sunshine after rain
(*Venus and Adonis*)

Love sought is good, but given unsought is better—Olivia (*Twelfth Night*, Act iii, scene 1)

MUSIC
If music be the food of love, play on—Orsino (*Twelfth Night*, Act i, scene 1)

Index

A

actors see players
Alchemist, The 57
alchemy 57
aldermen 30, 70
Alleyn, Edward (Ned) 33
apothecaries 29
apple-wives 44
Arcadia 54
archery 15, 70
Armada, Spanish 26, 64, 70
astrology 56
Aubrey, John 17, 49
audience 44–45

B

back-staff 57
bear-baiting 21
Beaumont, Francis 54
beauty 22, 43
Bible 10
birch beating 8
Blackfriars Theatre 54, 55
books 23, 60, 61
boy players 42–43
bull-baiting 20
Burbage
  James 32, 34
  Richard 33, 34, 50, 58

C

cannons 27, 35, 58
cartoons 62
Catholics 10, 11, 26, 70
christenings 16
clowns 38
cockfights 20
comedies 46–47, 65
Condell, Henry, 60
costumes, 32, 33,
  40, 43, 49
countryside 12–13, 14–15
courtiers 22, 23, 30
crops 13
crucifix (cross) 11, 70
cutpurses, 31, 45

DE

dance 32, 38, 39
Davis, John 57
Dee, Dr. John 56, 57
Dr. Faustus 25, 33
Earl of Essex (Robert
  Devereux) 23, 27
Earl of Southampton
  28, 65
editions, 61
Elizabeth I 10, 11, 15,
  22–23, 48
entertainments 14–15, 20–21

F

falconry 14
Falstaff 63
farm animals 12
fashion 29, 40, 41, 42, 55
fencing 50, 51
festivals 15
films 42, 47, 51, 57, 63, 65
First Folio 60, 65, 70
Fletcher, John 54, 58
flowers 13
Forbidden Planet 63

G

Galilei, Galileo 56
gallants 29, 41, 64, 70
galleons 27
gallows 20, 70
gambling 20
games 15
Garrick, David 63
gentlemen 31, 50
Gerard, John 60
Globe (modern theater)
  33, 58, 68, 69
Globe (original theater)
  34–35, 36–37, 44, 58
  heavens 35, 36
  thatched roofs 35, 58
  trapdoor 36, 37
glove-making 6
gloves 6, 14, 40
Greene, Robert 24, 25
groundlings 45
guilds 19

HIJ

Hathaway, Anne, 16, 59
Heminges, John, 60
Henry VIII, 10
History of Plants 61
history plays 26, 65
hornbooks 8, 70
hunting 14
Isle of Dogs, The 30
James VI of Scotland
  (James I of England) 48
Janssen, Geerart 59
jewels/jewelry 23, 40, 59
Jonson, Ben 25, 30, 52,
  57, 62
Julius Caesar 52

KL

Kemp, Will 32
King's Men 48–49, 54, 58,
  59
Kiss Me Kate 63
Kyd, Thomas 24
laws 17, 30, 40
London 18–19, 20–21, 30,
  31, 54
  Bankside 18, 34
  Bear Garden 21
  Church, St. Mary Overie's
  19
  Southwark Cathedral
  19, 62
  Staple Inn 19
Lord Admiral's Men 33
Lord Chamberlain
  (Henry Carey) 30
Lord Chamberlain's Men
  32–33
Lord Mayor of London
  30
Lord's Prayer 8

MNO

magic 25, 49, 55
makeup 22, 43
Mark Antony 52, 53
Marlowe, Christopher 24,
  25
Mary, Queen 10, 11
Mary Stuart, Queen of
  Scots 11
masques 55
maypoles 15
medicine 13, 17, 29
merchants 19, 44, 70
Metamorphoses 9
musical instruments 38, 39
musicals 63
Nashe, Thomas 24, 28

navigation 56, 57
noblewomen/men 14, 15,
  29, 43, 44, 46, 40, 42
operas 63
Ovid 9

P

patrons 28, 30, 48, 65
penknife 25
pens 9, 25
Philip II, King of Spain
  26
plague 28–29, 48, 70
platt (plot) 36
players 17, 22, 30, 32–33,
  36–37, 40
playhouses 20, 21, 28,
  30, 34–36
  gallery 44, 45
  gentlemen's rooms 44
  robberies at 31, 44, 45
  tiring (dressing) room
  33, 42
  yard 44, 45
plays (Shakespeare's)
*A Midsummer Night's
  Dream* 15, 47, 60,
  62, 67
A Winter's Tale 54, 66
All's Well That Ends Well 49
Antony and Cleopatra 53,
  67
As You Like It 8, 9, 40,
  42, 46, 67
Cardenio 58
Coriolanus 52, 66
Cymbeline 13, 54
Hamlet 13, 37, 50, 51, 65,
  66
Henry IV Part One 26, 39,
  64, 67
Henry IV Part Two 26, 67
Henry V 12, 26, 36
Henry VI Part One 32
Henry VI Part Three 14
Henry VIII 58, 62
Julius Caesar 52, 66
King John 11
King Lear 39, 50, 51,
  56, 57, 66, 67
Love's Labour's Lost 12
Macbeth 48, 49,
  50, 63, 66, 67
Measure for Measure 49,
  66
Much Ado About Nothing
  23, 40, 66, 67
Othello 50, 51, 63, 66, 67
Pericles 55

Richard II 26
Richard III 27, 67
Romeo and Juliet 14, 29,
  32, 50, 61, 63, 67
The Merchant of Venice 39,
  46, 66, 67
The Merry Wives of Windsor
  45, 46, 67
The Taming of the Shrew
  14, 39, 47, 63, 65, 66
The Tempest 54, 55, 57, 63,
  66
*The Two Gentlemen of
  Verona* 38, 46
Titus Andronicus 9, 24, 67
Troilus and Cressida 49, 67
Twelfth Night 39, 47,
  66, 67, 71
Two Noble Kinsmen 58
plays, staging 30, 36–37
playwrights 24–25, 52, 70
pocketbooks 61
poetry 23, 28, 50, 65
pomanders 28, 29
pressman 60
printers 60, 61
props 32, 33, 36, 37
Prospero's Books 57
Protestants 10, 11, 70
Puritans 11, 30, 60, 70

QR

quartos 60, 71
Queen's Men 17
Ralegh, Walter 23, 27
rats 28
reading 8–9
religion 10–11, 26
revenge tragedies 24, 71
Roman plays 52–53
romances 54–55, 71
rosary beads 10, 71
Rose Theatre 21, 35,
  44, 45
Rowe, John 16
ruffs 37, 40, 41, 71

S

saints 10, 11
schools 8, 9
Scottish play 49
scriveners 24, 71
Seaman's Secrets, The 57
Seneca 9, 52

serenade 38, 71
Shakespeare, John 6, 7,
  16, 17
Shakespeare, Mary 7
Shakespeare, William
  birthplace 6–7
  children 16, 59
  coat-of-arms 48, 61
  house (Blackfriars) 55
  house (Henley Street) 6
  monuments 59, 63
  wife 16
  will 59
Shakespeare Jubilee 63
Shakespeare in Love 42
Sly, William 32
songs 38
Sonnets 64, 65
Spain 26, 27
sports 14, 15, 20
stage hands 32
Starry Messenger, The 56
stinkards 45
Stratford-upon-Avon 6,
  58–59, 63, 69
  Hall Croft 59
  Holy Trinity Church 58, 59
  New Place 58, 59
street sellers 19
Swan Theatre 20, 21, 35, 36
swordfighting 50, 51

TUVW

Tamburlaine 25, 33
Tarlton, Richard 17
Thames River 18
Theater 21, 32, 34
tiremen 33, 42
tobacco 29
touchpieces 48
tragedies 9, 39, 50–51,
  65, 66, 71
tragic roles 33
traitors 18, 19, 20, 27
Tree, Herbert Beerbohm
  62
Verdi 63
watermen 18
weapons 36, 50, 51
Webb, Christopher 62
West Side Story 63
witches 48, 49
women's roles 42
wool 6, 16, 19, 41
writing 9, 25

Acknowledgments

Dorling Kindersley would like to thank: Models: Kate Adams, Annabel Blackledge, Ken Brown, Nick Carter, David Evans, John Evans, James Halliwell, Jamie Hamblin, James Parkin, Alan Plank, Dan Rodway, and Johnny Wasylkiw. Makeup artists: Jordana Cox, Hayley Spicer. Props: Ken Brown. Wigs: Darren and Ronnie at The Wig Room. Armorer: Alan M. Meek. Stylist: Judy Hill. Costumes: The RSC, Stratford. Editorial assistance: Carey Scott. Index: Lynn Bresler. Wallchart: Steve Setford and Peter Radcliffe.

For this relaunch edition, the publisher would like to thank: Hazel Beynon for text editing and Carron Brown for proofreading.

The publishers would like to thank the following for their kind permission to reproduce their photographs:
a=above; b=below; c=center; l=left; r=right; t=top

AKG London: 16tl, 20cl, 23br, 38bl, 39tr, 46bl, 51tl, 54cla, 54cl, 54br, 55cra, 57tl, 60tl, 61cl, 61bl, 63bc; British Library Add. 48027 Folio 650 11cr, Folio 57
Harley 1319 26cl; Erich Lessing 9clb, 38tl. Avoncroft Museum Historic Buildings: 34cl. Bridgeman Art Library: 71tl; Beauchamp Collection, Devon 27br; Belvoir Castle, Leicestershire, UK 65br; Birmingham Museums and Art Gallery 64cr; Bolton Museum and Art Gallery, Lancashire, UK 65tr; Bristol City Museum and Art Gallery, UK 55c; British Library 25br, 30bc, 60c; Christie's Images 61br; Collection of the Royal Shakespeare Theatre 67cl; Dulwich Picture Gallery, London, UK 32c; Dyson Perrins Museum, Worcestershire, UK 62tl; Fitzwilliam Museum, University of Cambridge 28cl; Guildhall Library, Corporation of London, UK 20–21, 55cl; Helmingham Hall, Suffolk, UK/Mark Fiennes 38cr; Linnean Society, London, UK 61tl; National Museums of Scotland 8b; Norfolk Museums Service (Norwich Castle Museum) UK 40br; Private Collection 11tl, 11bl, 28b, 30c, 36tl, 46cr, 54cr, 66bl; Private Collection/Barbara Singer 27tl; Private Collection/Christie's Images 16tr; Private Collection/Ken Walsh 24–25; Private Collection/The Stapleton Collection 23bl; Victoria & Albert Museum, London, UK 16r, 40bl; Walker Art Gallery

Board of Trustees National Museums & Galleries on Merseyside 22c; Yale Center for British Art, Paul Mellon Fund, USA 34tr, 46br. British Library: 4bl, 18–19, 23tl, 61tr, 61cr, 70b. © The British Museum: 11(main image), 18tl, 19tr, 49br, 52c, 56ca; Chas Howson 21tr. Christie's Images Ltd: 66bkg, 68bkg, 70cb, 70b, 71tc. Corbis: 64bl, 68tl, 68br, 69tr, 70t; Robert Estall 16c; Lebrecht Authors/Lebrecht Music & Arts 67 tr. Photographic Survey Courtauld Institute of Art: Private Collection 30tl. By permission of the Trustees of Dulwich Picture Gallery: 33tc (detail). Dulwich College: 36cl. Edifice: Gillian Darley 69bl. Museum of English Rural Life: 13tl. Mary Evans Picture Library: 8tl, 9cb, 12tl, 13br, 15tl, 15cr, 15bl, 17bl, 17bc, 19tl, 21tl, 22tl, 25tr, 29tr, 30clb, 30br, 32tl, 33tl, 48tl, 48tr, 48br, 54crr, 63t; Ames 56tr; Charles Folkard 55tl; ILN1910 44tl. Glasgow Museums; Art Gallery & Museums: 10tl, 11tr. Ronald Grant Archive: 47cr, 52tl, 52br, 53tc, 53br, 62cl, Prospero's Book © Allarts Enterprises 57br, Animated Tales of Shakespeare's A Midsummer Night's Dream © BBC 62c, The Winter's Tale 1966 © Cressida Film Productions 54tl, Forbidden Planet © MGM 63bl; Hamlet 1948 © Two Cities 51cl. Kobal Collection: 65bl, 66tr, 71b. Mary Rose Trust: 15tr, 27tc, 65tr. Museum of London Archaeology Service: Andy Chopping 45br. Courtesy of the Museum of London: 3, 10bl, 16bcl, 19bc, 22–23, 24br, 25tc, 34clb, 40cl, 48c, 59br.

National Maritime Museum, London: 26–27, 56–57b, 57tc, 57tr, 58bc, 64tr, 70r; Tina Chambers 20bcl. The Natural History Museum, London: 2bc, 37tr. The Picture Desk: Art Archive 67br. Post Office Picture Library: Shakespeare's Theatre Postage Stamps © The Post Office 1995. Reproduced by kind permission of The Post Office. All Rights Reserved 21tl, 21cl, 35tcl, 35tcr, 58br. Premier Brands: 26bl, 26br, 50tl, 50crb, 51tr, 51cr, 51bl, 51bll. Public Record Office: 59cl, 64bkg. Museum of the Royal Pharmaceutical Society: Jane Stockman 29cr. The Royal College of Music, London: Division viol by Barak Norman, London, 1692 39tl. St Bride Printing Library: 60–61. Science & Society Picture Library: 56bl. Science Museum: 48cl, 56–57c; John Lepine 28r. Shakespeare Birthplace Trust, Stratford-upon-Avon: 6cl, 6br, 6–7, 7bl, 7br; Malcolm Davies 10c, 60cl; By kind permission of Jarrold Publishing 6tl, 58tl, 59tl. Shakespeare's Globe: Donald Cooper 58cr; Nik Milner 32–33; John Tramper 37tl. Courtesy of the Trustees of the V&A Picture Library: 6bl, 40tl. Vin Mag Archive: SAC 42tl. The Wallace Collection: 26tl, 27tr. Warwick Castle: 36tr. Weald and Downland Open Air Museum: 7tr, 13c. Westminster Cathedral: 10cr. York Archaeology Trust: 24cl.

All other images © Dorling Kindersley.
For further information see: www.dkimages.com